The Urban Guide to Biblical Money Management

OTEIA BRUCE

**The African American Christian Publishing &
Communications Co.
1-800-860-8642
www.urbanministries.com**

Urban Ministries, Inc.
Chicago, IL 60643

*An independent African American
Christian Publishing Company
inspiring and empowering Christians
for over 30 years*

First Edition
First Printing
ISBN: 0940955-73-3

All Scripture references are taken from the New Oxford Annotated Bible, New Revised Standard Version (NRSV) unless otherwise noted.

Copyright © 2002 by Urban Ministries, Inc. All rights reserved. No part of this publication may be reproduced, stored in a retrieval system, or transmitted in any form or by any means, electronic, mechanical, photocopy, recording, or otherwise except for brief quotations in printed reviews without prior written permission from the holder of the copyright. Printed in the United States of America. Permission is given to photocopy the Appendix section of this book for personal use.

DEDICATION

*To my husband, George,
my children George III, Kayla and Dane.
My parents Harold and LaVonne Curington
and my Grandmother, Ann Crawford.*

TABLE OF CONTENTS

Foreword vi
Introduction vii
Acknowledgments viii

SECTION I — **Managing God's Gifts Faithfully (Matthew 25:14-30)**
Chapter 1 — The Point of Faithful Stewardship (Luke 19:15-26) 11
Chapter 2 — Financial Planning (Proverbs 6:6-11) 18

SECTION II — **Getting Your Financial House in Order (Proverbs 27:23-27)**
Chapter 3 — Budgeting for Bills and Dreams (Luke 14:28-30) 34
Chapter 4 — Credit Matters (Proverbs 22:1, 7) 51

SECTION III — **Building for Your Future (Proverbs 21:20)**
Chapter 5 — Bank and Stock Market Investment Instruments (Offline and Online) (Hosea 4:6) 73
Chapter 6 — Home Ownership and Investment Property Matters (Joshua 1:9-11) 102
Chapter 7 — Entrepreneurship Matters (Proverbs 22:29) 114

SECTION IV — **Sheltering Your Future (1 Timothy 5:8)**
Chapter 8 — Insurance, Wills, and Estate Planning Matters (Proverbs 13:22) 122
Chapter 9 — Tax Matters (Matthew 17:24, 27) 132

Glossary 139
Appendix 145
The Urban Guide Answer Key 156

FOREWARD

Oteia Bruce has written a much needed "How To" guide for Christians who are serious about being faithful stewards over God's resources. Unfortunately, most of what one hears and reads these days has nothing to do with the Word of God or the will of God. It is nothing more than the "American Dream" of how to get rich, how to prosper, and how to make money with no regard for any social consciousness or regard for those whom Jesus calls "the least of these." Thank God Mrs. Bruce's work is not like that.

To find a Christian woman who cares about others and who advocates money management that does not do violence to others is a rare find. Mrs. Bruce needs to be commended because of her care for God's earth, God's people, and God's kingdom.

Responsible investment, corporate responsibility in investment, and a Christian conscience are the over-riding principles that teach those of us who live in the city how Jesus would do it if He were alive in the 21st Century.

I thank God for her research and for her willingness to share the vision that God has given her.

Rev. Dr. Jeremiah A. Wright, Jr.
Senior Pastor, Trinity United Church of Christ
Chicago, Illinois

INTRODUCTION

So many have missed out on the financial plan that God originally designed for them due to fear, lack of knowledge, money mis-management, and more. The primary focus of this book is to help readers understand what the Bible has to say about our money management habits, consider common financial mistakes, how to avoid and recover from them, and discover how to build financial security for ourselves and families in God's way.

In writing this book, I wanted to stress that money management requires a commitment to educating yourself about money matters. It is not something you will generally learn in a school setting. I know people with very little formal education who have become multi-millionaires by applying simple principles of finance and money management to their lives, along with a lot of common sense. Some of them hire Ivy-League scholars to work for them. I also know people with MBA's and PH.D.'s who are struggling to make ends meet. This reinforces the fact that God has no respect of persons. As a result, for nearly two decades I have committed myself to training people at all levels about the subject of personal money management. It is my goal in this book to help you understand the various facets of handling money, matters both from a spiritual and natural perspective. After reading the principles outlined and practicing the assignments given, you will be prepared to change your financial destiny. I pray that you will take on the challenge.

This book has four sections, in which you will learn about everything from budgeting, credit repair, stock market investments, home-ownership, using the Internet to enhance your portfolio, and real estate investments to small business development, insurance selection, preparing your will, and much more. All sections and chapters start off with a scriptural reference that is used as a foundation to build and expand upon when covering financial concepts. Each chapter ends with case studies and/or questions designed to help you keep the material fresh in your mind. Please review continuously.

I pray for your financial success, and I hope that you will spread your success to others in your family, church, and community at large.

ACKNOWLEDGMENTS

Writing a book takes a village. It is no small undertaking to put nearly two decades of your life in writing in a way that is interesting and pertinent to others. Nor is it easy to write from a biblical perspective on the topic of finance without being pedantic and preachy, without the help of the village that is, people who are not afraid to say: "That's boring," "That's misspelled," "That's out-dated," "Stop talking about it and write it," "Girlfriend you need a break; you go girl." It also includes those people who said things like: "We'll be praying for your success," "Here's what to do to get a book deal," "We'll publish the book," "Don't forget your publishing deadline," "You've been typing past midnight too many times, it's time for bed," "Mommy, it's dinner time,".... What can I say? God has blessed me with a bountiful supply of very supportive village people, whom I love and appreciate dearly.

You may not know them, but because of their support for me you will come to know a lot more about money management. So, either now or in your leisure, please take time out of your schedule to read this section that acknowledges the people and institutions that made it possible for me to give something valuable to you.

Many, many thanks to the following: My husband for his patience, support, advice, prayers, and love; my children for their patience; my parents for their prayers, emotional, and moral support; Jeffrey Wright and Urban Ministries, Inc. for giving me the book contract; Dr. Okechukwu Ogbonnaya for his relentless support and guidance as my editor; Dr. Melvin and Mrs. Banks for having the vision and courage to start up and build the nation's largest African American Christian Publishing Company; my good friend, Ella Armstrong, who listened and prayed with me every step of the way and made me laugh when I got tired of typing, researching, and everything else; Cynthia Milsap, Director of the Night Ministry and (formerly of The DePaul University Egan Urban Center), who encouraged me to rejuvenate my long-term dream of writing this book; Mary Gotschall, writer for Fortune Magazine and co-writer of *It's About The Money*, by Reverend Jesse Jackson, Sr. and Congressman Jesse Jackson, Jr., who encouraged me strongly to complete this book; Kelvin Boston, author of *Smart Money Moves for African Americans*, and producer and host of PBS special "The Color of Money," who advised me numerous times on writing the book and how to get the contract; Garland Singleton, who welcomed me as the first African American female instructor at the Moody Bible Institute Extension Studies program; the Northwestern University Norris Center staff, who welcomed me as a Stock Market Investments instructor; and my grandmother, in her relentless pursuit to help others.

Section I

MANAGING GOD'S GIFTS FAITHFULLY

Matthew 25:14-30

[14] "For it is as if a man, going on a journey, summoned his servants and entrusted his property to them; [15] to one he gave five talents, to another two, to another one, to each according to his ability. Then he went away. [16] The one who had received five talents went off at once and traded with them, and made five more talents. [17] In the same way, the one who had the two talents made two more talents. [18] But the one who had received the one talent went off and dug a hole in the ground and hid his master's money. [19] After a long time the master of those servants came and settled accounts with them. [20] Then the one who had received five talents came forward, bringing five more talents, saying, 'Master, you handed over to me five talents; see, I have five more talents.' [21] His master said to him, 'Well done, good and trustworthy servant; you have been trustworthy in a few things, I will put you in charge of many things; enter into the joy of your master.' [22] And the one with the two talents also came forward, saying, 'Master, you handed over to me two talents; see, I have made two more talents.' [23] His master said to him, 'Well done, good and trustworthy servant, you have been trustworthy over a few things, I will put you in charge of many things, enter into the joy of your master.' [24] Then the one who had received the one talent also came forward, saying, 'Master, I knew that you were a harsh man, reaping where you did not sow, and gathering where you did not scatter seed; [25] so I was afraid, and went and hid your talent in the ground. Here you have what is yours.' [26] But his master replied, 'You wicked and lazy servant! You knew, did you, that I reap where I did not sow, and gather where I did not scatter? [27] Then you ought to have invested my money with the bankers, and on my return I would have received what was my own with interest. [28] So take the talent from him and give it to the one with ten talents. [29] For to all those who have, more will be given, and they will have an abundance; but from those who have nothing, even what they have will be taken away. [30] As for this worthless servant, throw him into the outer darkness, where there will be weeping and gnashing of teeth.'"

In addition to its spiritual message, the preceding Scripture has major implications for this life as well. Some ancient authorities say that a talent was equivalent to more than 15 years' worth of wages. Imagine that! If each servant earned $30,000 per year, the first servant would have received $2,250,000 and returned $4,500,000. The second servant would have received $900,000 and returned $1,800,000. The third servant would have received $450,000 and returned the same amount with no additional return. God will give us money and other gifts to manage. Whether great or small, when He provides for us, He expects us to do something with what He has provided.

Can you imagine a parent giving a child something they have pleaded for for a long time? Let's say it's a new car, gift-wrapped with a bow. Think about how astonished the parent would be if he or she had to unwrap the gift, throw away the paper, and put the keys in the ignition to start the car. After this, the parent then chauffeured the perfectly healthy child around town in the new car. Not only would the parent be astonished; he or she would be a whole lot of other things that I will refrain from saying in this book because it is a Christian publication. The parent could deal with this matter in several ways: return the car to the dealership promptly to get a refund, give it to another, more grateful child, or keep it for him- or herself.

> *"If you have stumbled along the road of money management, remember that God is a forgiver as well as a redeemer."*

Of course, this is an extreme example used to make a significant point. Have you ever felt like you missed out on something God had for you because you did not handle your money matters in quite the right way? Well then, this book is for you. God blesses us with many gifts, money being one of them. Along with the gift of money, He gives us an important task called responsibility. Whether we handle money on our own or seek professional advice, the final responsibility is ours. If you have stumbled along the road of money management, remember that God is a forgiver as well as a redeemer.

In this section we will cover "The Point of Faithful Stewardship" and "Financial Planning" in Chapters 1 and 2, respectively. We will cover what true wealth is and God's blueprint for how we should handle it. We will explore how we can get on track and stay on track with God's financial plan for our lives, as we study the lives of the faithful and unfaithful stewards in the Parable of the Ten Minas. We will also cover how to move forward if you are already on track, setting financial goals to achieve your dreams. Communication about finances is also one of the topics covered in this section, since it can be a major stepping stone or stumbling block, based on how we succeed or fail in this area. We will look at several productive ways to communicate with family and financial advisors as well as ways to choose a financial advisor.

Chapter 1

◆◆◆

THE POINT OF FAITHFUL STEWARDSHIP

This chapter will cover what the Bible has to say about true wealth, stewardship, the gift of money, and managing money from God's perspective. Our lives as faithful stewards should dictate our financial habits. Too often, we stray from God's design for stewardship; however, He is able to redeem us from the mistakes we make with money.

Four principles from the Parable of the Ten Minas illustrate the point of stewardship and how we can stay on track with God's financial plan for our lives.

Luke 19:15-26, NIV

[15] He was made king, however, and returned home. Then he sent for the servants to whom he had given the money, in order to find out what they gained with it. [16] The first one came and said, 'Sir, your mina has earned ten more.' [17] 'Well done, my good servant!' His master replied. 'Because you have been trustworthy in a very small matter, take charge of ten cities.' [18] The second came and said, 'Sir, your mina has earned five more.' [19] His master answered, 'You take charge of five cities.' [20] Then another servant came and said, 'Sir, here is your mina; I have kept it laid away in a piece of cloth. [21] I was afraid of you because you are a hard man. You take out what you did not put in and reap what you did not sow.' [22] His master replied, 'I will judge you by your own words, you wicked servant! You knew, did you, that I am a hard man, taking out what I did not put in, and reaping what I did not sow? [23] Why then didn't you put my money on deposit [in the bank], so that when I came back, I could have collected it with interest?' [24] Then he said to those standing by, 'Take his mina away from him and give it to the one who has ten minas.' [25] 'Sir,' they said, 'he already has ten!' [26] He replied, 'I tell you that to everyone who has, more will be given, but as for the one who has nothing, even what he has will be taken away.'

The message that God is relaying on in this Scripture passage is that what we do with what He has given us is of paramount importance to Him. Whether it is money, talent, time, etc., God truly expects us to sow it and reap a harvest for His kingdom. His kingdom includes ourselves, our family, friends, church, community, the nation, and the world. Your job in

God's kingdom may not be to save the world by reducing inflation or budget deficits in developing countries, however, you *do* have an assignment. It might only be establishing a budget for your household and increasing the amount you give to your church. No matter what our role in this life is: mother, father, homemaker, plumber, dentist, doctor, senator, truck driver, teacher, lawyer, corporate vice president, or CEO; we all have a responsibility to give an account of what we do with what God has given us. This book is a guide on money management. So let's focus on money and wealth and our ability to get and manage it.

Wealth today includes money, investments, land, and other assets that can be converted into cash. It also includes material goods, resources, property, and capital. **True wealth** includes all of the above plus all of the gifts, talents, and spiritual riches that God has given you. Wealth is described as an abundance of possessions or resources. During the times of the Patriarchs (Abraham, Isaac, and Jacob) wealth was measured largely in livestock sheep, goats, cattle, donkeys and camels. People in ancient times also measured wealth in terms of land, houses, servants, slaves, and precious metals.

> *"We are God's stewards, His managers, and God wants us to manage his gifts wisely."*

Stewardship is managing something that belongs to another. We are all stewards, and all that we have belongs to God. Everything we possess, own, have earned, worked for, invested, built, negotiated for, inherited, purchased, etc. belongs to God. Even though God has given us these things, they still unequivocally belong to Him. Yes, we may feel that our own ingenuity, the people we have met, the relationships we have built, and the knowledge we have gained through school, books, workshops, etc. are the main cause of our generating money and creating wealth. Yet this is not so. "Do not say to yourself, 'My power and the might of my own hand have gotten me this wealth.' But remember the Lord your God, for it is He who gives you power to get wealth" (Deuteronomy 8:17-18).

God is the one who gives others the knowledge to advise you, the ability to teach you, the power to promote you, and the influence to recommend you for higher positions. God is also the one who gives you favor with Himself and with others. "The earth is the Lord's and the fullness there of; the world, and they that dwell therein. (Psalm 24:1, KJV). We are God's stewards, His managers, and God wants us to manage His gifts wisely.

In the Parable of the Ten Minas (Luke 19:15-26), four things were used to express the point about stewardship: time, talent, money, and land.

1. Time—After leaving for a while, the king returned. How much time he gave to the servants was not stated, but some time was given. Isn't that just like God? He will come back to test us on what He has taught us without telling us when, and expect us to ace the test. If we do not pass, He will do us the heavenly favor of testing us again, again, and again. "For a righteous man falls seven times, and rises again" (Proverbs 24:16a). I don't know about you, but I don't want to take the same test several times.

For example: Your company was downsized and you did not save enough for your family's daily needs. You did not buy enough insurance to cover your medical expenses, and you recently had major surgery that was not fully covered by your current policy. Your son was accepted at an Ivy League college without a scholarship, and you did not invest in a college savings program for him. Or you went through a divorce and were left with the debts of your former spouse . . . oops! Many make these mistakes, yet do not learn a lesson the first time and continue down the same paths over and over again.

Yes, God can step in and miraculously provide for you in each of these situations. But just because He *can* does not mean that He always *will*. What He is ultimately looking for is for you to be prepared ahead of time whenever possible. Sometimes He will allow adversity in our lives to teach us. Use your time on this earth wisely.

2. Talent (ability and giftedness)—Though not explicitly stated in this Scripture, one would generally think that if a king takes time out of his busy schedule before going away on a trip to specifically select someone to manage his money, he must have some notion that that person has some talent to manage it. Of course, he also realizes that some stewards have more wisdom in this area than others. Yet, all have some wisdom, or the ability to ask someone else who has wisdom, or the ability to read about how to manage money, or the ability to take a class about matters of basic financial management before the king returns to see what has been accomplished. Many say, "I do not have the know-how," or, "God didn't give me a whole lot of money."

For example: How many of us took advantage of the American Century Ultra mutual fund that allowed investors to start with $1 and had 1 year in which it boasted a greater than 90% return on investment? This means that if you had invested $100 for 1 year, you would have had $190 at year-end. An investment of $1,000 would have grown to $1,900. An investment of $10,000 would have grown to $19,000 (Table 1.1).

Initial Investment	$100	$1,000	$10,000
1-Year Return on Investment at 90%	$190	$1,900	$19,000

Table 1.1 • Return on Investment

Where would one have gotten this information? While I understand that this information wasn't floating around on the billboards in our communities, neither did we have to go to the Library of Congress to do extensive research. The information was right in our midst at the local grocery and drugstore on the magazine rack, in *Money Magazine* and *Kiplinger's Personal Finance*. God can take the little talent we have and turn our reading and taking action into phenomenal results.

Sometimes, using some of the gifts and talents we take for granted in a slightly different way can produce extraordinary results. For example: the talent of reading can be focused on regularly reviewing materials that cover basic financial principles. The more regularly we use reading to increase our knowledge of financial matters, the more proficient we become as wealth and investment managers. Even when you commit to reading financial materials for only 15 minutes daily or even weekly, it is like making a direct deposit into an account that will ultimately build a wealth of knowledge allowing you to build your portfolio. *Money Magazine*, *Kiplinger's Personal Finance*, *Investor's Business Daily*, *Fortune*, and *The Wall Street Journal* are excellent publications in which to make your reading investment.

> *Sometimes, using some of the gifts and talents we take for granted in a slightly different way can produce extraordinary results.*

The gift of television is no different. Of the time you spend watching television, how much time do you spend watching programs that cover financial news, money management, and other financial matters? When you couple reading information with viewing programs that focus on personal financial matters, you are promoting a marriage made in heaven as far as your money is concerned . . . not to mention adding the "offspring" of various financial workshops, web sites, books, and other media that exist today, helping you along in your financial journey. Television programs such as "Ahead of the Curve" and "Power Lunch" on CNBC, web sites such as MSN Money Central, MSNBC, Investor's Business Daily (America Online and WSJ.com), and *The Wall Street Journal's* web site offer extremely valuable information.

3. Money (Mina)—A mina was a unit of currency equal to 3 weeks' worth of wages at the time this parable was written. Think of someone today earning $1,000 per week and God giving them $3,000 to manage. As the master did in the Parable of the Ten Minas, God has used money in both large and small amounts to teach us, reward us, and show His awesome glory in our lives . . . not just for our benefit, but for the benefit of others in our families, churches, communities, jobs, and in the world at large.

Recall the story of Joseph, a lad who had little more than a dream, a loving father, and, at that time, conniving brothers who left him for dead in a pit and then sold him into slavery. God took Joseph from the pit and the prison to the palace and the pinnacle of success as a head of state in a foreign country. God did not elevate Joseph and give him wealth just for himself. He did this so that Joseph could save the people in the surrounding countries, including his family (and those conniving brothers) from the famine. Even more, God wanted to fulfill His promise to Israel (Jacob), Isaac, and Abraham that He would multiply their seed and make them more numerous than the sands on the seashore.

Of the three stewards to whom the king left money in the Parable of the Ten Minas, two of them returned to the king a greater amount than he gave them initially. He considered them faithful and rewarded them accordingly for investing his money wisely. However, the last steward was severely punished because he did not invest the king's money at all. The money he had been given was quickly taken away and given to one of the other stewards who had invested. Today many people suffer in this way, only today their money is being taken away quickly and given to their creditors. The creditors are the stewards who have been getting the money of those who have not been wise managers of the money God has given to them.

4. Land—In return for managing their money wisely, the two servants received land from the king, who appreciated their diligence in reaping an increase on the amount of money originally given to them. In return for their investing his money, the king gave each servant cities. The first steward received ten cities for reaping a tenfold return on the king's money, and the second steward received five cities for reaping a fivefold return on the king's money.

Throughout the Old Testament, God used possession of land as a way to reward His people. He knew that the possession and control of land was a physical way of showing power. Those who possessed land were usually the greatest in the earthly kingdoms and had the greatest armies and the greatest inventories of livestock, grain, and other resources. They were able to generate more revenue through trading with the vast amount of resources at their disposal.

What was the last steward thinking? Even if he had earned just one more mina than he received, he would have been very well off financially. He would have been given at least one city. I'll take that! How does the reward given in this parable translate into today's terms? Well, what does real estate ownership mean today? How does God use real estate to empower you? Similar to owning land back in biblical times, real estate is usually the largest asset that an individual will purchase or own in his or her entire life.

God can use real estate to empower you in various ways, especially in three important areas: appreciation, increased income, and tax reduction.

Appreciation is powerful because it represents the growth in the value of an asset over time. In eight years, I have seen my own property value more than triple. That's better than the stock market! This phenomenon is enjoyed by property owners across the board, and some individuals' property values grow at an even faster rate.

Increased income comes into play when you rent part of your property to others. Many do this through the purchase of investment property. Additional income is a wonderful source for making investments in other assets, like CD's, money markets, mutual funds, and more real estate.

Tax reduction is a third advantage of real estate ownership. Real estate not only gives you a roof over your head, but also makes it possible for you to reduce your taxable income. Property taxes paid to the county in which you reside can be deducted from your gross income.

Summary

In this chapter, we have studied the Parable of the Ten Minas. Even though the parable only gives the results for three of the stewards to whom the minas were given we discussed how it relates to us today and how God uses this parable to illustrate the importance of faithful stewardship in our lives. By studying this parable, we examined how God can use time, talent, money, and land to teach us, bless us, and show His awesome power in our lives and the lives of others around us. We also discussed our roles as faithful stewards and the true value of wealth.

Take a look at the following review questions. Discover how well you remember the concepts discussed and how much you have used the principles of biblical stewardship in your own life.

Questions

1. What is true wealth?

2. What assets did the faithful stewards reap for investing the money given to them by the king?

3. What asset in today's times is likened to the commodity given to the stewards as a reward?

4. How can we benefit from this asset?

5. What four things were used in the Parable of the Ten Minas to illustrate the importance of faithful stewardship?

6. How were these four things used to make the point?

7. What is stewardship?

8. What are some of the ways God can use money in our lives?

9. How did God use Joseph as a faithful steward?

10. How has God used adversity in your life to bless and teach you?

11. How has God used money in your life to bless you and others?

12. How have you used your talent and time to reap benefits for the kingdom of God?

13. In what ways can you invest your time, talent, money, and land (if applicable) to become a more faithful steward in your personal financial life?

Chapter 2

◆◼◆

FINANCIAL PLANNING

This chapter will discuss the importance of financial planning; including setting short-term, medium-term, and long-term financial goals. The importance of incorporating dreams into the goal-setting process and determining one's needs, wants, and desires will also be discussed. Ways of reaching the goals we set will be covered through case studies that focus on setting dates and assigning dollar amounts to each dream and goal. This chapter will also cover choosing a financial advisor(s) and successfully communicating your financial goals to your family, significant other, and financial advisors (CPA's, bankers, brokers, etc.).

Proverbs 6:6-11

⁶ Go to the ant, you lazybones; consider its ways, and be wise. ⁷ Without having any chief, officer or ruler, ⁸ it prepares its food in the summer, and gathers its substance in harvest. ⁹ How long will you lie there, O lazybones? When will you rise from your sleep? ¹⁰ A little sleep, a little slumber, a little folding of the hands to rest, ¹¹ and poverty will come upon you like a robber, and want like an armed warrior.

A **financial plan** is a working document used to map out our goals and strategies we will use to achieve them. Your financial plan can be as flexible or as firm as you need it to be. Some develop a simple financial plan on their own. Others use advisors, software, financial web sites on the Internet, etc. An actual financial plan prepared by an advisor could include your budget, statement of net worth, education plans, retirement plans, life insurance, business plans, estate plans, wills, and trusts.

Whichever route you decide is best for you, remember that it is very important to set dates and a dollar amount for each goal that you have; otherwise, the financial plan is really nothing more than a dream or fantasy on paper.

Financial planning helps you define your goals in terms of dollar amounts and time frames. We must separate our goals based on how soon we need to achieve them; otherwise, we run the risk of mis-prioritizing. This can cause us to allocate most of our savings and investments to only one or a few goals and miss out on building for other things we need in life. In the area of retirement savings, many would get an A or B grade because most of us have a company pension plan, 401(k), or some other plan that automatically deducts money from our payroll check. We usually find out about these plans the first day on the job. It is made very simple for us to start. However, when it comes to setting up a regular savings or investment plan for our short-term needs, many of us would receive a less desirable grade.

A financial plan is a working document used to map out our goals and strategies we will use to achieve them.

Often, our short-term savings and investment goals require that we seek and act on investment information on our own. This is a more cumbersome job than having information continually dropped into our laps by our employers in the form of payroll stuffers. It is fine to save for retirement as a primary goal, because many value steady income at retirement as a high priority. As long as we do not forget to put away savings for other major goals e.g., a down payment on a house, tuition, vacations, a new car, etc. it's all good.

Goals fall into three main categories as far as time is concerned: short-term, medium-term, and long-term.

1. Short-term goals are goals that need to be achieved in 1 year or less. Examples include: a down payment on a house or car, reducing expenses on a budget statement to qualify for more house, paying off all creditors, attending a family reunion, taking a vacation mid-year, etc.

2. Medium-term goals are goals that need to be achieved in 1 to 5 years. Examples include: saving for child care expenses; private grammar school, high school, or college tuition; a dream vacation; returning to school; starting a small business; remodeling your home; etc.

3. Long-term goals are goals that can be achieved over a longer period of time (6 years or more). Examples include: retirement planning, relocating to another state, buying a vacation home, purchasing a boat, etc.

How you prioritize your goals largely depends on what stage of life you are in. For example, education may be a short-term goal for some and a long-term goal for others. A new car purchase may be a mid-term goal for some, while it can be a short-term goal for others. Your income, number of dependents (children, parents, spouse, or others), marital status, age, debts, monthly expenses, assets (savings accounts, CD's, investments, real estate, etc.), insurance, trusts, wills, etc., will be the determining factors in setting the timelines for your goals.

Needs, Wants, Desires and Dreams

Another key element in goal setting is establishing one's needs, wants, and desires. Distinguishing between these three areas of our lives can help us avoid problems as we try to prepare a financial plan or make financial decisions. Most people have a pretty good idea of where to draw the line, but there are times when even the most disciplined person can get off track. Many have faced the challenge of maintaining clear lines between each category. Let's review the categories:

Needs are basic day-to-day necessities, such as food, shelter, clothing, and health insurance.

Wants are things one purchases to enhance the quality of life. These things usually vary in cost and quality depending on one's budget. They may include transportation, clothing, housing, furniture, dining and entertainment, travel, etc. For example: One person may purchase a coat from Sears while another may choose to purchase one from Nieman Marcus. One person may choose to bring lunch to work daily, another may choose to eat at the employee cafeteria, and yet another may eat daily at a gourmet cafe. One person may choose to commute to work via public transportation, another may choose carpooling, and still another may choose to drive daily. As you can see, these choices really depend on individual preferences and budgets.

Desires are things we choose that also enhance the quality of life but usually transcend the things we typically want in terms of price and magnitude. They can include (but are not limited to) taking dream vacations to exotic and interesting places like Hawaii, the Napa Valley, Morocco, Kenya, the Virgin Islands, Paris, London, Japan, Greece, etc.; attending major events such as the Olympic Games, Wimbledon tennis matches, the Super Bowl, the NBA playoffs, the Saratoga horse races, the Presidential Inauguration, and New Year's Eve in Times Square; making major purchases such as an expensive car, mansion, ranch, fur coat, etc.; being accepted or having one's children accepted at an Ivy League school, completing one's own college education, or obtaining a master's degree or Ph.D.; transitioning into an executive level position at one's company or building one's small business into a multi-million dollar company; and pastoring one's own church. This list could go on and on.

Dreams Before goals become goals, they generally exist as dreams. Dreaming is a very important element in the goal-setting process. While we may not be able to turn every dream into a goal, we should make a serious effort to pursue some of our dreams. Otherwise, our list of goals becomes merely a rigid, boring tool that relegates us to providing only for the basic necessities of life. Your first list should be a dream list, detailing as many needs, wants, and desires as you can come up with. Of course, you must modify your list. However, the beauty of this assignment is that you do not have to give up on your list. You can add your dreams to your list of goals as your resources grow. Before a dream becomes a goal, you must assign a date and a dollar amount to it.

Let's look at how to put together a goal matrix (Tables 2.1 and 2.2). Developing a goal matrix is one of the key starting points when preparing a financial plan.

Today's Date: _____

GOAL	AMOUNT NEEDED		DATE NEEDED
	Total	Monthly	
Retirement			
Financial Independence			
College Education			
Pay Off All Debt			
Major Purchase			
Significant Change In Lifestyle			

Table 2.1 • A Simple Goal Matrix

Remember that Table 2.1 is a simple goal matrix and you can add as many categories as you like. The categories are based on your own personal situation. Table 2.2 includes more details.

To help you, we will also look at three different scenarios involving individuals with a fixed amount of resources and time. In the following examples, no interest will be included for simplicity's sake. Total dollar amounts will be divided by the number of months one has to save for a specific goal.

GOAL	Year 1	Year 1-5	Year 6-10	Year 11-30
Paris Trip				
New Home				
Pay Debts				
Income Property				
Child Care				
Fur Coat				
New Business				
Charity				
Other				
Other				

Table 2.2 • A Detailed Goal Matrix

Mary Ward's Financial Goals

Mary is in her last semester of law school. She has a $6,000 tuition bill to pay before she can participate in the graduation ceremony in 6 months. Meanwhile, she just received a $90,000 job offer from the firm where she currently works as a part-time law clerk. She could start after she graduates and successfully completes the state bar exam. Her current part-time job pays $1,500 per month. She has no savings and her parents are on a fixed retirement income, which is too small for them to help her. She also has $60,000 of student loan debt she must repay. Last week, Mary's friends asked her to join them on a short trip to Jamaica right after graduation. None of them had gone on vacation since they started law school. The total cost of the trip is $1,500 (air, lodging, taxes, and meals). Mary really wants to go on this trip.

Mary receives a stipend that covers part of her tuition and living expenses. She has $1,000 per month left over after expenses, and leads a very active social life that consumes most of her money. She has also managed to save $3,000 in a savings account.

What do you think Mary should do? Change her lifestyle in the short run? Put away money to pay off her student loan? Forget about the trip to Jamaica? Let's look at her current situation in Table 2.3.

GOAL	AMOUNT NEEDED		DATE NEEDED
	Total	Monthly	
Tuition	$6,000	$1,000	6 Months
Jamaica Trip	$1,500	$250	6 Months
Student Loan	$60,000	$715	7 Years*

*Mary has the option to wait until up to 18 months after she graduates to start making minimum monthly payments of $715 on this loan.

Table 2.3 • Mary's Goal Matrix

Mary's Decision

Mary knew that she could either increase her hours on the job or decrease her spending for the next 6 months to cover the additional amount she needed for the trip. She found that it would be extremely complicated to increase her work hours during the time when she needed to study for finals. She therefore decided to drastically cut her spending so that she could put away an additional $750 per month to pay off her tuition and save for the trip to Jamaica. She decided that she would use the $3,000 in her savings to pay half the tuition. Then she would need to save only $500 per month to pay off the balance. An additional $250 would go toward the trip to Jamaica, leaving her with $250 to spend or save. She also decided to postpone the monthly payments of $715 on her student loan until after she finishes school.

GOAL	AMOUNT NEEDED		DATE NEEDED
	Total	Monthly	
Tuition	$3,000	$1,000	6 Months
Jamaica Trip	$1,750	$250	6 Months
Student Loan	$60,000	$0	7 Years*

*Mary will make no payments on the student loan for approximately 18 months. Once she starts, it will take 7 years (84 months) to pay it off with the minimum monthly payment of $715.

Table 2.4 • Mary's Adjusted Goal Matrix

Mr. and Mrs. Smith's Financial Goals

John and Kendall Smith are the parents of two small children who will be starting preschool in 1 year. The children are 1 and 2 years old. Kendall's mother will be relocating out of town and will no longer provide free child care. The Smiths want to save for preschool as well as for grammar school, high school, and college tuition and expenses. They would also like to purchase a new van in 1 year to help them transport their children. Preschool will cost $4,000 per year for each child. If the children attend public grammar and high schools, the cost to cover both children will be a total of $300 per year. If they attend private schools, the total cost will be $20,000 per year. The cost of a new van will be $30,000, with monthly payments of approximately $750 per month. College will cost $40,000 per child.

GOAL	Year 1	Year 1-5	Year 6-10	Year 11-30
	Annual/Monthly*	Annual/Monthly	Annual/Monthly	Total/Monthly**
Pre-School	$8,000/$667			
School-Public		$300/$25		
School-Private		$20,000/$1,667		
College-4 Yr.				$80,000/$393
New Van		$750		

*__Annual/Monthly__ refers to the annual and monthly amounts needed to accomplish short-term and medium-term goals. The total annual dollar amounts needed were divided by 12 to get the amount needed per month to achieve each goal.

**__Total/Monthly__ refers to the total and monthly amounts needed to achieve long-term goals. The total cost of a four-year college education was divided by 204 months (17 years x 12 months) to determine the monthly amount needed to pay for an education for two children at $40,000 per child.

Table 2.5 • The Smith's Goal Matrix

GOAL	Year 1	Year 1-5	Year 6-10	Year 11-30
	Annual/Monthly*	Annual/Monthly	Annual/Monthly	Total/Monthly**
Pre-School	$8,000/$667			
School-Public		$300/$25		
College-4 Yr.				$80,000/$393
New Van		$750		

Table 2.6 • The Smith's Adjusted Goal Matrix

The Smith's Decision

Mr. and Mrs. Smith will research various scholarship programs for all levels of education for their children in order to cut some of the education costs. Meanwhile, they must plan to save the amount necessary to accomplish their goals. They decide to send their children to public schools until college. They will purchase a new van at a dealership that requires no money down.

Dan Greenwich's Financial Goals

Dan Greenwich is a mid-level manager who has seen the company downsize and lay off many of his colleagues. Even though he recently received a new 4-year employment contract from his company, he plans to start his own web-based business in 2 years with money from his stock fund. He also plans to relocate to a warmer climate in 5 years. Business start-up costs will be approximately $15,000. The down payment on a new home in the region he is interested in moving to will be $20,000, with closing costs of about $10,000. Relocation costs will be $3,000.

GOAL	AMOUNT NEEDED		DATE NEEDED
	Total	Monthly	
New Business	$15,000	$624	2 Years
New Home	$30,000	$1,250	2 Years
Relocation	$3,000	$125	2 Years

Table 2.7 • Dan's Goal Matrix

Dan's Decision

While Dan has enough in his stock fund to cover costs, he is concerned about withdrawing money because he will lose his return on investment and will have to pay taxes. He therefore decides to set up a separate savings plan through his employer, with $2,000 per month being deducted from his paycheck. He will use the money in the stock fund after starting his business. This will allow him to receive tax deductions for business start-up costs and property ownership that will offset the taxes he will pay for withdrawing money from his tax-deferred stock fund.

Dan's adjusted goal matrix (Table 2.8) will remain the same as the goal matrix shown in 2.7 because he is able to start saving immediately toward his 2-year goal of $48,000 with a monthly payroll deduction of $2,000.

GOAL	AMOUNT NEEDED		DATE NEEDED
	Total	Monthly	
New Business	$15,000	$624	2 Years
New Home	$30,000	$1,250	2 Years
Relocation	$3,000	$125	2 Years

Table 2.8 • Dan's Adjusted Goal Matrix

Communication

Communication is the glue that will keep all of one's financial planning together and on track. With bankruptcy at an all-time high, widespread financial discord, and 50% of all marriages ending in divorce due to financial havoc, we cannot afford to fail to communicate. Think of it this way: the less we talk, the more we pay. You do not have to be a rocket scientist to communicate about your dreams, goals, and finances.

"The less we talk, the more we pay."

Start with the easiest thing first: your dreams, whether great or small. What dreams do you have? How many of your dreams have you achieved? How close are you to achieving unaccomplished dreams? Most people like dreaming and will be more than happy to discuss this part of their financial lives. Many spouses find it difficult to discuss finances. Dreaming together without criticism helps you realize that you are on the same team. Then it is easier to move to the next category: goals. When setting goals, it is necessary to brainstorm about the actual dates and dollar amounts needed to achieve dreams and to review plans that you have already put on paper and started to work on.

Discussing available finances is usually the most challenging part of communicating, which is why it should be approached delicately. Sometimes we do not have the luxury of going through this exercise. Many times we have to discuss finances now. Just remember, however, that the more frequently we use this communication model, the more likely we feel we are discussing our finances with a partner versus an antagonizer who wants to tear down our dreams.

Remember to follow the communication model:

• Discuss your plans and objectives in this order:
   1) Dreams
   2) Goals
   3) Finances

• Schedule a periodic review of your plans with the following individuals:
   - Yourself
   - Financial Planner/Consultant
   - Spouse (if applicable)
   - CPA
   - Children (if applicable)
   - Stockbroker

• Remember to set a reasonable review time that is neither too frequent nor too infrequent. Too-frequent reviews can cause irritation, while too-infrequent review scan cause financial emergencies that you might not overcome, or that may cost you more because you did not handle them in a timely manner. Depending on your objectives, monthly, quarterly, or semi-annual reviews/discussions could work.

Choosing An Investment Advisor

Ten things you should do when choosing an investment advisor:

1. Collect a list of candidates.
You can generate a list from friends, banks, brokerage companies, etc.

2. Meet at least three people from your list.
Take time to go to their place of business to see how well established or how reputable they are and how they interact with you. A nice location does not indicate competence, but it does give you some idea of how successful the advisor is in his or her field.

3. Ask each candidate for references.
Ask for a short list of three or four clients who have used the advisor's services. Also check with the local Better Business Bureau.

4. Pay attention to his or her title, but not too much.
Working with an advisor who has a big title is nice. Be aware, however, that some advisors have received higher titles because they sold a lot of products, not necessarily because they matched clients with appropriate investments.

5. Check the advisor's background.
How many years of experience does the advisor have working with clients who have a financial situation similar to yours? Experts say that 10 years is not too much to expect.

6. Do not trust a person just because he or she is a friend or relative.
Take your friends and relatives through the same evaluation process as you would a stranger, unless you are already familiar with their background. They should meet the same criteria that you require anyone else to meet. Failure to follow this process could be costly.

7. Ask how the advisor will be paid.
Advisors are usually paid in one of three ways: commission, flat fee, or fee plus commission. Because of the competition in the financial industry, investment professionals are more wary about making sure they suggest the right investments for their clients no matter whether they earn high commissions or not. The Securities and Exchange Commission (SEC) regulates investment sales activity nationwide. Still, be very cautious.

8. Ask how much the advisor will be paid.
Some advisors get a percentage of what they sell you. Ask about the fees associated with each investment you purchase; in some cases, there may be alternatives that cost less but have the same or better performance historically.

9. Have the advisor explain how the investments that he or she recommends will help you achieve your goals. You want an advisor who is willing and able to explain how investments can work for you and how they will fit into your portfolio.

10. Ask your advisor to explain how you will determine if your investments are producing the results you need. After making an investment, you should automatically receive a monthly statement in the mail giving you the status of your account. As suggested earlier, you and your advisor should review your account on a regular basis to evaluate performance and to determine if any changes should be made.

- **Remember to pay close attention to your own financial affairs, no matter who you choose as your advisor.**

Summary

In this chapter, we have covered:

- Financial planning and the various elements it takes to put together a good financial plan
- The importance of dreaming and determining one's needs, wants, and desires
- How to turn one's dreams into reality by setting goals with dates and dollar amounts on a goal matrix
- The importance of communication
- How to go about communicating your financial plan and with whom you should periodically review your plan
- Ten things to do when selecting a financial advisor

Questions

1. What creature did God use to teach us about planning ahead? Why?

2. What is a financial plan?

3. What is the difference between a need, a want, and a desire? Give examples.

4. What is the difference between a dream and a goal?

5. What are short-term, medium-term, and long-term goals?

6. What are the steps one should follow when communicating about finances?

7. Who should you communicate with regarding your finances?

8. How often should you communicate about your finances?

9. What steps should you take when choosing a financial advisor?

10. Who has the greatest responsibility for your finances?

11. You are relocating to Arizona in 3 years. The down payment and closing costs on your new home will be $10,000. The start-up cost for your new business will be $4,000 in 3 years. Use one of the matrices below to chart your goals.

GOAL	AMOUNT NEEDED		DATE NEEDED
	Total	Monthly	

GOAL	Year 1	Year 1-5	Year 6-10	Year 11-30
	Annual/Monthly*	Annual/Monthly	Annual/Monthly	Total/Monthly**

12. You will need a new car in 2 years, and you can afford monthly payments of $400. Your daughter will need braces in 1 year at a cost of $1,750. You will return to school in 3 years at the cost of $20,000 per year for 4 years. Your employer offers 50% tuition reimbursement. Private school for your daughter will cost $3,000 per year starting in 4 years. Use one of the matrices below to chart your goals.

GOAL	AMOUNT NEEDED		DATE NEEDED
	Total	Monthly	

GOAL	Year 1	Year 1-5	Year 6-10	Year 11-30
	Annual/Monthly*	Annual/Monthly	Annual/Monthly	Total/Monthly**

32 | The Urban Guide to Biblical Money Management

Section II

GETTING YOUR FINANCIAL HOUSE IN ORDER

Proverbs 27:23-27

[23] *"Know well the condition of your flocks, and give attention to your herds;* [24] *for riches do not last forever, nor a crown for all generations.* [25] *When the grass is gone, and new growth appears, and the herbage of the mountains is gathered,* [26] *the lambs will provide your clothing, and the goats the price of a field;* [27] *there will be enough goat's milk for your food, for the food of your household and nourishment for your servant-girls."*

Before we can move forward financially, we must know where we stand economically. The preceding Scripture points out that we should know what's going on with our household finances. How much we have, how far it will carry us, and how much we need to supply for our future welfare and that of our families is of utmost importance. Being able to provide financially on an ongoing basis and keeping tabs on what we already have are a function of how we manage the budget and credit process. It is very challenging to be spiritual when we don't have our earthly house in order.

In this section, we cover "Budgeting for Bills and Dreams" and "Credit Matters" in Chapters 3 and 4, respectively. How to prepare a budget and balance sheet will be discussed in this section. Analyzing and balancing the budget will be covered, as well as paying oneself first and building net worth. We will also outline the steps necessary to clear up one's credit history, avoid or recover from bankruptcy, stop aggravating creditor calls, and much more.

Chapter 3

◆◆◆

BUDGETING FOR BILLS AND DREAMS

This chapter will cover preparation of the income and expense statements the balance sheet, analysis of income and expense categories how to manage them, approaches to debt management, and avoidance and debt reduction. The focus will be on balancing the budget, and creating a surplus, paying oneself first, determining and building net worth, analyzing asset and liability categories, and asset management.

Luke 14:28-30
28 For which of you, intending to build a tower, doesn't first sit down and estimate the cost to see whether he has enough to complete it? 29 Otherwise, when he has laid a foundation and is not able to finish, all who see it will begin to ridicule him, 30 saying, 'This fellow began to build and was not able to finish.'

The Income and Expense Statement (Budget)
Now that we have had the chance to dream, we have to deal with the day-to-day job of handling our budget. A **budget** is a tool that you use to manage your daily financial activities. It serves as a guide that shows you what road you must take every month to get to your financial destination. When we stray from the road by overspending, we can use our budget as a road map to help us get back on track. Some people use their budget as a strict guide from which they will never stray, while others build in flexibility for additional spending. However, we must remember that the budget is a tool and not a weapon, much like a hammer. We can use a hammer to help us drive in nails to build or as a weapon to help us tear down. We must be careful with a hammer, and we must be careful with our budget. Keep your budget as simple as possible. Let's look at a monthly budget (income and expense statement) and analyze the categories.

INCOME & EXPENSE STATEMENT

Month _____

INCOME		**EXPENSES**	
Payroll	_____	Taxes	_____
Commission	_____	Tithes	_____
Bonus	_____	Investments/Savings	_____
Savings	_____	Mortgage/Rent	_____
Investment	_____	Auto	_____
Rental	_____	Credit/Loans	_____
Business	_____	Child Care	_____
Other	_____	Food/Groceries	_____
Other	_____	Clothing	_____
		Transportation	_____
		Insurance	_____
		Medical	_____
		Payroll Deduction	_____
		Toiletries	_____
		Recreation	_____
		Miscellaneous	_____

TOTAL INCOME _____   **TOTAL EXPENSES** _____

SURPLUS OR DEFICIT = INCOME − EXPENSES _____

Table 3.1 • Monthly Budget

Fixed and Variable Income and Expenses

In every budget you will find fixed and variable categories. It is important to keep track of these categories, because failure to prepare can create major emergencies and unnecessary embarrassment. In addition, it is important to track how frequently expenses are paid and income is received, e.g., biweekly, monthly, quarterly, annually, or sporadically. Table 3.2 lists some categories of income and expenses.

FIXED INCOME	VARIABLE INCOME	FIXED EXPENSES	VARIABLE EXPENSES
Payroll	Commission	Mortgage/Rent	Credit/Loans
Rent	Bonus	Auto	Food/Groceries
	Savings	Taxes	Child Care
	Investment	Tithes	Toiletries
	Business	Payroll Deduction	Entertainment

Table 3.2 • Sample Income and Expense Categories

Some of these categories can be either fixed or variable depending on your situation (e.g., child care, credit, loans, bonuses, etc.). Just remember to use a monthly average for categories that vary. Sporadic bills or income should be added in the months they occur. If you know when to anticipate them, you should plan by putting them into your budget. Also remember to plan for the tax consequences of any sporadic income so that you can save accordingly. We will look at examples of budgeting for sporadic income and expenses later in the chapter.

Weekly, Biweekly	Payroll, income taxes
Monthly	Payroll, income taxes, commission, mortgage, interest
Quarterly, Semiannually	Bonuses, insurance, property tax, dividends
Annually Sporadically	Bonuses, income tax Dividends, capital gains, royalties, etc.

Table 3.3 • Income and Expense Frequency

Budget Category Analysis

Analyzing your budget categories and how much you spend in each category is key to having a successful financial plan. The purpose for analyzing or reviewing your budget is to see if you have actually stayed on track with your financial goals. Additionally, this exercise gives you the ability to look at the details of how you are spending your money, because you actually look at the separate components that make up the budget categories. After analyzing the separate components of your budget, you can map out the necessary changes on your own, with a spouse, and/or with a financial planner. Let's review each of the budget categories, some of their components, and the ways that we can manage them to our benefit.

Income Categories

Fixed Sources of Income

Payroll and **rent** are generally fixed sources of income that are not as flexible as other sources. They usually change very gradually with an increase in salary or the purchase of new property. Of course, some opt to lease out space in their homes or apartments to generate additional income for a given period of time. If you are very familiar and comfortable with the person(s) you are leasing to, this is a great way to generate additional income to pay off debts or invest for your future.

Variable Sources of Income

Variable income usually changes to some extent. Because these sources of income are flexible, they give us the opportunity to create more wealth, pay off more debt, and improve our quality of life. This depends on how disciplined we are in following our financial plans and how serious we are about managing what God has given us. This is what separates the wealthy from the "unwealthy." Let's review some sources of variable income.

A **commission** is a source of income that one can use to finance anything, e.g., debt reduction or payoff, education, dream vacations, etc. The biggest challenge that many face is remembering not to get so elated about the additional income that they spend it all. Depending on the commission structure and the person's commitment to hard work, that person could literally raise him or herself to a higher financial status. Some earn commissions through additional part-time work or in their full-time positions.

"The biggest challenge that many face is remembering not to get so elated about the additional income that they spend it all."

A **bonus** is usually a subjective source of income for those in upper management and sales positions: the bonus is based on the employee's individual performance and the company's overall performance. However, it is up to management's discretion as to whether these funds will be paid out. Some employees receive bonus checks representing a certain percentage of their salary. Others receive fixed dollar amounts. Whatever the case, the rule is still the same: pay down as much debt as possible and/or invest in your future. Remember your set of short-term, medium-term, and long-term goals.

Savings are usually generated through depositing money in bank instruments. These generally pay a fixed interest rate, with the exception of money market accounts, which fluctuate gradually with market rates. Bank instruments generally pay lower rates than non-bank investments, yet they provide the most safety as far as loss is concerned. They are insured by the Federal Deposit Insurance Corporation (FDIC) for up to $100,000 per account owner. While bank instruments pay a lower rate of return, they are a necessary part of your portfolio for cash reserves, emergency funds, daily living funds, and other short-term cash needs. You should have funds that you can withdraw immediately or within a very short period of time to meet short-range planning needs. These funds may be kept in vehicles such as checking or savings accounts, money market accounts, and certificates of deposit (CD's). Note that the term of investment for CD's can range anywhere from 7 days (at some banks) to 10 years. Checking accounts, money markets, and savings accounts are flexible accounts which you can withdraw money at any time by check, teller withdrawal, ATM, or debit card withdrawal.

> "The rule is still the same: pay down as much debt as possible and/or invest in your future. Remember your set of short-term, medium-term, and long-term goals."

An **investment** is one way to pay yourself with income generated by a variety of financial tools. These could include (but are not limited to) stocks, bonds, mutual funds, options, futures, real estate investment trusts (REIT's), and precious metals. Stocks, bonds, and mutual funds come with various levels of risk. They can range from very safe, income-oriented instruments with little or no fluctuation in price, to moderately yielding income and growth instruments, to aggressive growth instruments that give you the opportunity for the highest level of return but with the highest risk of losing your investment. Options, futures, precious metals, and REIT's are some of the riskiest investments available. While they offer the possibility of generating extremely high rates of return (e.g., 100%, 200%, 500%, 1000%, or more), they are not designed for the average investor. One must be extremely savvy about the markets to take advantage of these types of investment instruments.

Investments are an important part of a financial, because they have historically out-performed bank instruments. While they are an excellent source of income, choosing the right investment(s) is very challenging. Either you or an investment advisor must do the research to find the right mix of investments to meet your financial goals. (We will cover investments in more detail in Chapter 5.)

A **business** represents a source of income generated from your entrepreneurial efforts. Many find this income source easier to grasp than previous sources. Because one can run a business part-time in addition to having a regular job, it is an excellent way to generate income to pay off debts and save for the future. Some opt to run their businesses full-time because it gives them more income and flexibility than they would have working as an employee for a company. (We will cover this more in Chapter 8.)

Other income is a catch-all category for all other sources of income, which could include tips, royalties, baby-sitting fees, etc. Many people are being very creative when it comes to generating extra income. As economic times bring corporate downsizing, benefit cutbacks, salary freezes, and uncertainty, it is extremely important to know how to do more than one job. Learning new skills or brushing up on old ones may be your link to financial security.

Expense Categories

Fixed expenses are payments made over time that remain constant for the duration of a contract, e.g., mortgages, rent, insurance, auto loans, equity credit loans, and other consumer loans. They can also be a constant percentage of one's income, e.g., taxes, tithes, and payroll deductions. Making larger payments toward these loans or paying them off in full can be a major financial benefit. As you pay off debts, you can use the additional funds to invest or pay off more debt.

"Thereby put me to the test, says the Lord of hosts, if I will not open the windows of heaven for you and pour down for you an overflowing blessing."

There is very little one can do to reduce the amount of **taxes** that are withheld from one's salary. However, those who make large charitable contributions and run home-based businesses are able to receive large tax deductions. Small business owners can deduct all business expenses from gross income. This can allow a substantial reduction in one's year-end tax bill or create a large tax return.

Tithes are the Christian's way of giving to God what He asks. Ten percent of our income is all God asks of us, even though 100% of it belongs to Him. As we are faithful in our tithes and offerings, God opens more doors for us. He asks us to make Him prove Himself in Malachi 3:10: "Bring the full tithes into the storehouse, that there may be food in my house, and thereby put me to the test, says the Lord of hosts, if I will not open the windows of heaven for you and pour down for you an overflowing blessing."

For some, it is no problem at all to set aside income to pay tithes and offerings. For others, it can be a struggle because their income barely covers the bills that are due. What should one do in this case? Some may choose to give the total amount of tithes and offerings due monthly, quarterly, or semiannually when they receive large commissions or bonuses. Whether we decide to give every pay period or on some other periodic basis, it is imperative that we give what God asks if we really want to receive His full blessings in our lives. It is not always easy. This is a **major** test of faith. There is no other way to describe it.

Insurance is an expense that generally remains stable. It should change only with increasing or decreasing family needs for coverage. Some use it as a tax-deferred way to save for college education for their children and retirement for themselves. They do this by paying an additional amount on top of their regular insurance premium.

Payroll deduction is usually an amount taken out of one's paycheck as a percentage of income or a fixed dollar amount. This is an effective way to make tax-deferred investments for retirement and other goals. Of course, income taxes, Social Security taxes, etc. are deducted also.

Automobile loans have payments that remain constant. Some people work extra hours, extra jobs, or in their part-time business to pay off auto loans before they are due. Some opt to use the car in their business and take tax deductions for mileage accrued. The only way to know which option is best for you is to speak with a tax advisor. The age of the car will play a big role in the advice you receive.

Variable Expenses

Whichever investment or savings instruments you decide to use in your portfolio, it is very important to pay yourself first. You should invest 10% of your income if possible; if you are not able, then try 5%, 3%, or some fixed amount. You can always choose to increase the amount of your investments later. Setting up an automatic debit from your bank account to a mutual fund or some other investment vehicle is the best way to build your investments. This is a convenient way to accomplish your goal without having to remember to do it yourself every pay period or so. Treat yourself like a creditor, and you will reap the financial reward.

Other variable expense categories are subjective. The best strategy is to avoid spending unnecessarily, especially if you are trying to stick to a budget to achieve certain goals. These variable expenses are usually the areas where drastic overspending takes place. We can use several excuses to justify increased spending on clothes, entertainment, groceries, and toiletries. However, these are expenses that we must control with all diligence. Miscellaneous expenses are another area that we must watch closely.

Budget Analysis

Budget analysis gives you the chance to review your activity in each category as well as make changes in your spending or savings habits where necessary. In Table 3.4, there are four columns that you must complete. Column 1 identifies the budget items. Column 2 (Projections) shows the spending and income projections for the month. If you do not have any idea what to put in this column, look at your prior month's income (paycheck stub) and bills (billing statements). This will give you an idea of what expenses and income should be placed in this column. Column 3 (Actual) shows the amounts that you actually spent and brought in as income. You may have to keep a notepad to record these items every time you spend, then transfer the total to your budget at the end of the month. Column 4 (Difference

+/-) shows the difference between your projected income and expenses and the actual amounts earned and spent. If any of the categories show zero or a negative balance, you need to make some changes soon. Even if the numbers are positive, you can still make changes, such as reallocating your surplus to save more toward your financial goals. Once you have recorded everything, subtract expenses from income to find out how much money you will have left over at the end of the month.

Total Monthly Income − Total Monthly Expenses = Money Available

Budget Items	Projections	Actuals	Difference (+/−)
Payroll	_____	_____	_____
Commission	_____	_____	_____
TOTAL	_____	_____	_____

EXPENSES

	Projections	Actuals	Difference (+/−)
Taxes	_____	_____	_____
Tithes	_____	_____	_____
Investments/Savings	_____	_____	_____
Mortgage/Rent	_____	_____	_____
Auto	_____	_____	_____
Credit/Loans	_____	_____	_____
Child Care	_____	_____	_____
Food/Groceries	_____	_____	_____
Clothing	_____	_____	_____
Transportation	_____	_____	_____
Insurance	_____	_____	_____
Medical	_____	_____	_____
Payroll Deduction	_____	_____	_____
Toiletries	_____	_____	_____
Recreation	_____	_____	_____
Miscellaneous	_____	_____	_____
TOTAL	_____	_____	_____

Table 3.4 • Budget Analysis

The last thing we must remember about budgets is that most categories have subcategories that vary depending on how we spend our money. Table 3.5 shows some of these subcategories.

Investment/Savings	Taxes	Credit/Loans	Clothing
Emergency Fund Education Fund Cash Reserve Retirement Savings (Separate from payroll-deducted employer plans)	Income Property	Installment Loan Equity Loan Credit Cards Line of Credit Student Loan	New Purchases Dry Cleaning
Auto	**Insurance**	**Medical**	**Payroll Deductions**
Payment Maintenance Gas Parking	Life Medical (Non-employer) Auto Property Casualty	Prescriptions Co-pay	401(k) Pension Savings Plan Stock Options Medical Insurance Life Insurance Accident Dental
Entertainment	**Transportation**		
Movie/Theater Travel/Vacation Dining Recreation	Bus/Train Cab		

Table 3.2 • Sample Income and Expense Categories

The Balance Sheet

The balance sheet shows us our net worth at a specific point in time. We can review what we *own* and what we *owe* with this statement. Once you know the balance of your assets (what you own) and the balance of your liabilities (what you owe), you can begin to make the changes you need to increase your net worth (assets vs. debts). The dollar amounts reported on the balance sheet should be the total amounts owned or owed, not the periodic amounts paid or deposited in the monthly budget.

Assets (What You Own)

There are various categories of assets that we need to cover to better understand the balance sheet. These include: cash assets, investment assets, personal assets, and real estate assets.

Cash assets are cash or cash equivalents that you can access immediately on a short-term basis. They include checking or savings accounts, money market accounts, money market funds, CD's, Treasury bills, and the cash value of some insurance policies.

Investment assets can include but are not limited to stocks, bonds, mutual funds, REIT's, precious metals, IRA's, 401(k)'s, pensions, and annuities. Some investment assets are more long-term than others, such as retirement assets.

Personal assets represent the personal property that you own. They can include cars, jewelry, furniture, appliances, home office equipment, boats, coin collections, and antiques. Some of these assets are considered investments because they can appreciate over time (e.g., jewelry, coin collections, and antiques). Other assets lose their value (depreciate) over time. assets that depreciate include cars, boats, office equipment, appliances, and other items.

Real estate assets obviously include your home, investment property, and vacation home. Real estate is an asset that can add value in various ways. You can use it, rent it, lease space in it, and sell it. It can serve as a physical shelter, a tax shelter, an income-producing investment, a net worth builder on your balance sheet, or a source of profit when you sell it.

Liabilities (What You Owe)

Liabilities (debts) fall into two main categories: short-term and long-term. Generally, short-term debts are anything that must be paid off in 1 year or less. Long-term debts are those that can be paid off over longer periods of time.

Short-term (current) liabilities include credit cards, lines of credit, personal loans, margin loans (loans made to you through your stock brokerage company to purchase more securities), and property taxes. Although property taxes are automatically paid out of the escrow you build when you make your monthly mortgage payments, it is still important to keep track of the amount owed on your balance. Property taxes are usually due quarterly. Treat this category just like credit balances that are being paid down with automatic debits from your checking account.

Long-term liabilities include mortgage loans, auto loans, student loans, business loans, and other loans. These are loans that you pay off over years in monthly installments.

Net Worth (Assets–Liabilities)=What You're Worth

Net worth represents what you would be worth if you paid off all your debts today with available assets. Please remember that this has nothing to do with your spiritual condition, although it may reflect some spiritual disconnectedness from God and His plan for your life. To some, it may be disappointing to review their balance sheet because the bottom line is lower than they would prefer, or even negative. The good news is that net worth is a number that can be manipulated in your favor if you will just stay on track with God's financial plan for your life.

Let's take a look at a sample balance sheet in Table 3.6.

BALANCE SHEET

Date _____

ASSETS		LIABILITIES	
Cash (Reserve) Assets		**Short-Term Debts**	
Checking	_____	Credit Cards	_____
Savings and Money Markets	_____	Lines of Credit	_____
		Personal Loans	_____
Cash Value of Life Insurance Policy	_____	Margin Loans	_____
		Property Taxes	_____
Investment Assets			
Stocks, Bonds, and Mutual Funds	_____	**Long-Term Debts**	
		Auto Loans	_____
Retirement/ Keogh Accounts	_____	Student Loans	_____
Pension/401(k) (Vested)	_____	Mortgage Loan	_____
		Business Loans	_____
Personal Assets		Other	_____
Car	_____		
Furniture and Appliances	_____		
Jewelry, Other	_____		
Real Estate			
Home	_____		
Investment Property	_____		
Other Property	_____		
TOTAL ASSETS	_____	**TOTAL LIABILITIES**	_____

NET WORTH (Total=Assets−Liabilities) _____

Table 3.6 • Balance Sheet

SPECIAL NOTE: When preparing your budget (income and expense statement) and balance sheet, it is important to remember to make room for an emergency fund. An unprecedented number of employees at all levels have experienced corporate downsizing. Even though the United States has had amazing economic growth and low inflation, several of its stalwart industries have laid off tens of thousands of employees to keep themselves globally competitive.

The computer, high-tech, and auto industries have suffered the most. To stay afloat, they have transferred jobs overseas, where labor is inexpensive; they have merged with other companies; and they have put their companies on the selling block. I mention all of this because it is important for you to be prepared not scared. Prepared with an **emergency fund** to see you through any tough times you may experience. Remember the ant! How much should you save in an emergency fund?

Many financial planning experts recommend that 6 months' salary be set aside for those in salaried positions and 12 months' income for those in commission-based positions. But having experienced corporate downsizing, seeing how time off ravaged my savings, and knowing that economic downturns hit urban America much harder than anywhere else, I would make the following recommendation to you as a financial advisor: Save 12-24 months' worth of your employment income whether you are commissioned or salaried. The more the better! Your time out of work might last longer than 6 months, or you may end up taking a lesser-paying position that does not generate enough income to cover your bills.

How long should it take me to save this amount in my emergency fund? I thought you would ask that! Remember that not everyone will be able to save at the same rate because their financial circumstances and/or personal situations are not the same. First, review all of your goals, your budget, and your balance sheet. Then determine where and by how much you can decrease spending or increase income. Next, choose what asset(s) you want to invest in. Be patient. It could take several years to achieve your goal. Some choose the stock market because it has historically outperformed other investments since its inception in 1926. Stocks do not give a guaranteed return, but over time the stock market has proven to be a stellar performer. Because the stock market grows at a faster rate, it takes less time and money to achieve your goal. Choosing lower-yielding investments will usually involve less risk, but it will take longer to reach your goal. What you choose is based on your personal situation. (We will cover investment selection in Chapter 5.)

Questions

1. What does the monthly budget show?

2. Name five income or expense categories that are fixed and five that are variable.

3. Why is it important to keep track of expenses that occur at different frequencies (e.g., monthly, quarterly, or semiannually)?

4. What steps are necessary to calculate a budget surplus or deficit?

5. What are income and expense subcategories? Give five examples of each.

6. What three primary things does the balance sheet show?

7. What are the four main categories of assets on a balance sheet?

8. What are the two main categories of liabilities on a balance sheet?

9. How do you calculate net worth?

10. What is an emergency fund? What categories on the income and expense statement and the balance sheet might one increase to build an emergency fund?

11. Bob and Daisy Jackson need to save $300 more per month for their trip to Africa at the end of the year. In what category (or categories) can they cut spending, and in what category should they save the money? Make any needed changes on their budget which follows.

INCOME & EXPENSE STATEMENT (BUDGET)

Month __January__

INCOME		EXPENSES	
Payroll	$9,000	Taxes	$3,000
Commission	_____	Tithes	$900
Bonus	_____	Investments/Savings	$1,000
Savings	$200	Mortgage/Rent	_____
Investment	$500	Auto	$200
Rental	$300	Credit/Loans	$1,000
Business	_____	Child Care	_____
Other	_____	Food/Groceries	$1,000
Other	_____	Clothing	$1,000
		Transportation	$100
		Insurance	$300
		Medical	$100
		Payroll Deduction	$600
		Toiletries	$200
		Recreation	$400
		Miscellaneous	$150

TOTAL INCOME $10,000   **TOTAL EXPENSES** $9,950

SURPLUS OR DEFICIT (INCOME – EXPENSES) $10,000 $9,950 = $50

12. Bertha Johnson is concerned about paying a high interest rate on a new mortgage. With a higher down payment of $20,000, she can get a near prime interest rate. Use a plus (+) or minus (−) sign to identify the categories on her balance sheet that she should increase or decrease to achieve her goal.

BALANCE SHEET

Date _____

ASSETS		**LIABILITIES**	
Cash (Reserve) Assets		**Short-Term Debts**	
Checking	_____	Credit Cards	_____
Savings and Money Markets	_____	Lines of Credit	_____
		Personal Loans	_____
Cash Value of Life Insurance Policy	_____	Margin Loans	_____
		Property Taxes	_____
Investment Assets			
Stocks, Bonds, and Mutual Funds	_____	**Long-Term Debts**	
		Auto Loans	_____
Retirement/ Keogh Accounts	_____	Student Loans	_____
Pension/401(k) (Vested)	_____	Mortgage Loan	_____
		Business Loans	_____
Personal Assets		Other	_____
Car	_____		
Furniture and Appliances	_____		
Jewelry, Other	_____		
Real Estate			
Home	_____		
Investment Property	_____		
Other Property	_____		
TOTAL ASSETS	_____	**TOTAL LIABILITIES**	_____

NET WORTH (Total Assets − Liabilities) _____

Chapter 4

◆◆◆

CREDIT MATTERS

This chapter will cover eight steps to credit freedom, including how to use your credit wisely and keep your credit history clear. It will also cover how to control compulsive spending, compare various forms of debt repayment, avoid pitfalls, stop aggravating calls from collectors, negotiate with creditors and collectors, clear up your credit history, avoid bankruptcy or recover if you have already filed, and how to get free professional advice.

Proverbs 22:1, 7
1 A good name is rather to be chosen than great riches, and favor is better than silver or gold. 7 The borrower is servant to the lender.

The Scripture selected for this chapter focuses on character, favor, and position. A "good name" refers to the value of one's *character*. We are being exhorted to maintain good character in all that we do: with our finances, in our home, at work, etc. We are reminded that our character is so valuable that riches can't even compare with it. *Favor* is just as important to have. The favor of God and man is placed above the value of silver and gold. Without favor, it would be very challenging to get anything done that involves other people. Finally, the preceding Scripture focuses on the *position* of the borrower compared with that of the lender. Verse 7 does not discourage borrowing. It simply shows that the decision to borrow puts one in a position of financial and physical servitude; the person has no choice but to get up and go to work to pay off his or her creditors. How long one chooses to stay in this position is up to that person. Being on the "other side of the coin" (a lender) is obviously a much more desirable position to be in.

Throughout their lives, many people strive to attain the highest possible levels in all three areas: character, favor, and position. One of the most tangible ways to achieve these goals is through sound financial management and maintaining good credit. When you are unencumbered by debt, you have the freedom to chart your own financial path. While most people are not independently wealthy and must use credit to assist them in reaching their goals, we all must remember that credit can be used either constructively or destructively. Credit is another one of those tools that can be used to tear down or build up. God's will is that we build our futures on the foundation He has already laid. How we manage credit affects how others (creditors, collectors, etc.) judge our character. It can also determine how much favor we have with God and man. It can even determine the level and position which we attain in financial stability, on the job, in ministry, etc.

> *"The eight steps to credit freedom will show those who are on the right track how to keep pace and those who aren't how to get on the right track."*

Some of you are already wondering, "Well, what about me?" Perhaps you did not overspend using credit. Your creditors were not paid because you lost your job and suffered long-term unemployment, or you were left with all of the bills after a divorce, or you had unexpected medical bills from a long-term illness. Not everybody falls into the category of a compulsive spender. Credit issues can arise from all sorts of circumstances, even for those who are favored by God, who have outstanding character, and who are also in high positions spiritually, financially, vocationally, intellectually, or politically.

Think about Job. What if he were living today? He'd probably be moving in the same circles as the high-society muckety-mucks: mayors, governors, senators, influential ministers, or corporate and global leaders. He'd probably be one of those savvy people on the "A" list, invited to various events at the White House, one whose advice is sought out consistently by other business icons. Then all of sudden, KABOOM! Everything is gone. Imagine it! He has lost all of his children, his wealth, and his health due to natural disasters or so he thinks. He cannot bury his children decently because his insurance policies have expired. His cattle business has folded, so he can't generate income that way. Most of his wealth has been absorbed through lawsuits because he couldn't deliver on the contracts he made. The remaining money was spent on exorbitant medical costs for his terminal illness. He certainly can't get a job, considering how sick he is. He has lost his position, favor, and reputation with man even with his closest friends *but he didn't lose anything with God.*

Do you feel like Job when it comes to your credit situation? Well, there is good news. Whether your credit reflects a Job-like experience in your life, happy-go-lucky compulsive spending habits, stellar money management and wisdom, or somewhere in between, this chapter is for you. The eight steps to credit freedom will show those who are on the right track how to keep pace and those who aren't how to *get* on the right track.

Step 1: How to Use Credit Wisely and Keep Your Credit History Clear

It doesn't take a rocket scientist to figure out the formula for keeping one's credit history in good standing: pay your creditors on time. Yet it takes very strong self-discipline to follow this simple formula. Credit can impact so many areas of our lives, such as owning a home versus renting, driving a car versus taking public transportation, being hired for and/or promoted at a job, selecting a college for our children, or maintaining our family's financial stability and our ability to give to ministry. Our credit situation can even impact our health and our image of ourselves.

"Check your credit history periodically."

Here are a few suggestions that you can use to keep your credit history clear:

- Pay bills in a timely manner.

- Check your credit history periodically with all three credit reporting agencies (Trans Union, Equifax, and Experian [formerly TRW]). Sometimes they insert incorrect information on credit reports. You will need to write them to correct the erroneous information. We will cover how to do that later in the chapter.

- Pay more than the minimum monthly amount due. This looks great on your credit history and gives you negotiating power when you need more credit.

Step 2: How to Control Compulsive Spending

Many times, people spend compulsively because they feel they've earned it, worked hard for it, waited long enough for it, are worth it, are getting back at someone for doing something they didn't like, are depressed about various situations in their lives, learned this behavior from someone they admired, etc. In most cases, they *have* earned it. Yet when this criterion is used continually to justify our overspending, we wind up giving ourselves something we *don't* deserve, no savings and a ruined credit history. The novelty of the newly purchased items soon wears off, and we are left holding the unwanted bills.

Here are six suggestions to help avoid compulsive spending:

1. Don't ignore problems when they arise; deal with them swiftly.
Overspending on credit doesn't start off as a big problem; it occurs a little at a time. If not dealt with, it can become a very destructive force in our lives, our marriages, and other areas. Sometimes people who are in good financial shape ignore the warning signs because they know that they have been responsible with credit, then gradually wind up with excess debt. Others plunge into habitually using credit for everything and suffer grave financial consequences in the end. Nip this type of behavior in the bud, and you will resolve many of your credit challenges.

2. Set aside a reserve fund to help avoid overspending.
Spending extra cash that was not budgeted can have a major impact on your ability to

maintain good credit. It may not be very noticeable at first, but over time it can lead to huge budget deficits. Once all of the extra cash has been spent, some people have the ability to put on the brakes, but others don't. After the cash is gone, they use credit to assist them in their compulsive habit of overspending.

> *"True joy doesn't come from purchasing items, it comes from God. Every time you get the urge to spend, review your list."*

A reserve fund should be a bank account that is separate from your daily operating account so that you will stick to your limit. A reserve fund does two things: it gives you the flexibility you need to go on your shopping sprees, and it saves you the expense of overloading your credit cards. "The clever see danger and hide; but the simple go on, and suffer for it" (Proverbs 22:3). Correcting this problem immediately will save you a lot of grief in the future.

3. Avoid replacing needs with wants and desires when shopping.
When you see that item you've just got to have right now, even though you haven't budgeted for it, wait 2 to 3 weeks before you purchase it. Check other stores to see if you can get a better price. Give yourself time to build up some cash reserves to buy it. Later, this item will probably not be as much of a priority as you thought it was, assuming you still remember it at all. Simply by waiting, you have saved yourself from a "budget buster" and possible credit calamity.

4. Use a grocery list and try to avoid shopping for food when you are hungry.
It is amazing how much stuff ends up in the grocery cart during our trips to the store when we don't plan ahead of time. The more often you use a shopping list, the less likely you are to overspend using cash and/or credit.

5. Try to avoid shopping to get over depression or disappointment.
It is no secret that many people shop to relieve their depression, and they carry their best shopping buddy along with them; the credit card. They subsequently find out that the relief is short-lived and are right back to the same problems they had before they went shopping. In addition, they've got some extra credit card debt to accompany them in their depressed state.

Instead of shopping, find other activities you enjoy and/or seek professional help. Additionally, write down how spending your money on unnecessary items hinders you financially and emotionally and how saving this money will help you. True joy doesn't come from purchasing items, it comes from God. Every time you get the urge to spend, review your list.

One exercise that has helped me over the years is to go *window shopping only!* Sometimes I look at small-ticket items and sometimes at large-ticket items. I can remember the $100,000 Russian sable coats I've tried on, the Jaguar I test-drove, the $35,000 bed I bounced on, etc., etc., etc. I remember later taking the sales persons' cards and telling them I'd think about it. The truth is, *I did* think about it, right before I came to my senses. (Hey,

I've earned it!) Try it, you just might like it, and it just may help you get beyond some disappointment or depression.

CAUTION: If you are highly susceptible to purchasing small- or big-ticket items out of your budget, leave your credit cards and checkbook at home. Take only a limited amount of cash with you!

6. Avoid chasing dreams without sound plans.
Many people have fallen into the trap of investing or borrowing for some multimillion-dollar business idea, stock investment, new phenomenon extraordinaire, the eighth wonder of the world, etc. Of course, the sales person told them that it was important to get in on this marvelous opportunity right away and that prolonging their decision could cost them huge profits. Without sound information or the knowledge to thoroughly evaluate what they were getting into, they took the plunge. Not only did they invest time, energy, and money, but many of them financed these investments with credit. They used credit cards, home equity loans, loans from their retirement plans, high-interest loans from finance companies, and loans from relatives.

I often think about the people I know who have negligently invested in real estate, vacuum cleaners, vitamins, restaurants, music deals, boxes of bricks, pyramid marketing schemes, etc. Some of these investments may have been right for someone else, but not for them. If you are not able to research the matter enough or get sound financial advice from a professional, a member of your family, and/or one of your friends, walk away from the deal. Proverbs 11:14 says, "Where there is no guidance, a people falls, but in an abundance of counselors there is safety." (We will discuss sound investing in Chapter 5.)

Step 3: How to Compare Various Forms of Debt Repayment and Avoid Pitfalls

1. Additional Employment
Whether it's additional hours at work, a part-time job, using your hobby to generate income, or a small business venture; finding additional employment is one of the least costly ways to generate more money to pay off debts. However, one must consider the cost to oneself in terms of stress, conflicts with family commitments, or full-time job commitments, etc. Some families have allowed their teens to work part-time to help out. Make sure that you build flexibility into your schedule so that you don't miss out on the quality time you need for yourself and your family. Additionally, one should count the monetary cost. It costs money to go to work or run a small business. Consider additional costs for transportation, child care (if applicable), income taxes, supplies/inventory, clothing, food, etc. After you have considered all the costs, you might find that you could wind up just breaking even or even losing money.

2. Family and Friends

Borrowing from family members is one of the least expensive ways to get money to pay off your debts. You can avoid a lot of paperwork and the hassle of having to prove your creditworthiness. However, there is one caveat: Put this loan agreement with your relative in writing, listing the total loan amount and the time within which you will pay it back. If periodic payments are necessary, note how much you will pay back periodically. Also make a note if any interest is to be included. Sign and date this document. Your family member or friend will respect you more for taking this business-like approach, and you will be more likely to get the loan because they can see how serious you are about paying them back.

3. Employee Savings Plan Loans

Loans from a corporate savings or investment program are easy to get as long as you have built up funds above a specified minimum level and can show some hardship as a reason for the withdrawal. The interest rate is usually very low, and the money is paid back into your savings as you make payments to the employer. You are actually paying yourself back. This account is not a normal bank account. It is set up through your benefits department as a payroll deduction. The payments that you make to cover your loan will be automatically deducted from your paycheck on a periodic basis. Call your employer to find out if this program is offered and what the specifics are.

"Borrowing from family members is one of the least expensive ways to get money to pay off your debts."

4. Insurance Policy Loans

Insurance policy loans are low-interest loans that are easy to get if you have a whole life or universal life insurance policy. You can borrow from the cash value. With a current insurance policy, you can pay off the loan over longer periods of time. If you die before the loan is paid off, your beneficiaries will receive the cash benefit minus the principal and interest you owe.

5. Consolidation Loans

Consolidation loans are made by banks to pay off your debts. The interest rates on these loans are usually lower than credit card rates. Because you must use collateral to protect the interests of the bank, the bank assumes less risk, so your rate is lower. If you default on the loan, the bank gets your collateral. Keep these payments current.

6. Credit Unions

If you belong to a credit union through your employer or another organization, you have access to lower interest rates on personal loans. Credit unions are known for charging lower rates to their members because of the relationship you have with your employer or participating organization (union, church, etc.).

7. Bank Personal Loans or Lines of Credit

The personal loans and lines of credit made available by banks carry slightly higher interest rates than the previously mentioned alternatives. Loans are made for a fixed amount, while lines of credit give you a flexible account into which you pay a monthly minimum just like with a credit card loan. Interest rates on lines of credit are slightly higher than personal loan rates. One must be very careful not to use the line of credit to make other purchases when trying to consolidate debts. If one is unable to qualify due to a poor credit rating, the bank may suggest using a co-signer who has a higher credit rating. Be sure to make timely payments on all loans and lines of credit, especially with a co-signer. Late payments will negatively impact the credit history of the co-signer.

8. Home Equity Loans

Home equity loans are made based on the amount of equity in your home (current market value of your home *minus* the amount owed on your mortgage). The equity in your home serves as collateral. The interest rates are usually lower than with other types of bank loans if you have stellar credit. You will also receive a tax deduction for the interest you pay up to a certain limit as determined by the IRS. Just remember that if you default on the loan, you could lose your home.

9. Finance Companies

Finance companies are owned by groups of private investors who are willing to take greater risks than a traditional bank. They provide more flexible lending alternatives. In exchange for assuming higher levels of risk, they charge a higher interest rate and require collateral. Yet the rate is usually lower than some high-interest credit card rates. Finance companies are not regulated by banking commissions.

10. Sub-Prime Lenders

Below-prime lending companies loan money to individuals with slightly to extremely negative credit histories (sometimes including bankruptcy). When there is nowhere else to turn, people call on these lenders to help them in the short term. Unfortunately, some people keep long-term loan arrangements with these lenders and wind up paying exorbitant amounts of money for funds they borrowed. These lenders consist of some banks, finance companies, and mortgage companies. Because they assume extremely high risk, they charge much higher rates. In some cases, the rates they charge are higher than credit card rates. This practice is known as *predatory lending* and is being closely scrutinized and outlawed by a growing number of states. If the rate you are quoted by this type of lender is close to or higher than credit card rates, try some of the other strategies covered in this chapter.

"If you must do business with a sub-prime lender, make sure your loan term is as short as possible."

CAUTION: If you must do business with a sub-prime lender, make sure your loan term is as short as possible. Make accelerated payments to pay off your loan sooner. Once you clear up your credit history, try getting a loan with another lender that charges lower rates and pay off the balance.

Step 4: How to Stop Aggravating Calls from Collectors

As a consumer, you have rights that are protected by the Fair Debt Collection Practices Act passed by Congress in 1977. This act prohibits certain types of debt collection methods. Writing a **cease-and-desist** letter is the key to legally stopping aggravating calls.

A cease-and-desist letter is written to the collection agency to notify them that they are not to contact you any more. Once they have received this letter, they cannot contact you, except to inform you that they will not contact you any more or that specific actions will be taken against you. This applies to all forms of creditors: collection attorneys, independent collectors, and collection agencies. Take into account that this letter might speed up legal action because the account could then be passed on to an attorney. If you are able to negotiate with creditors before it gets to this point, do so.

Things collection agencies *cannot* do:
- Harass, oppress, or abuse any person
- Use obscene or profane language
- Repeatedly use the telephone to annoy a person
- Call inconveniently before 8 a.m. or after 9 p.m. unless you agree
- Falsely imply that they are an attorney or government representative
- Misrepresent the amount of debt you owe
- Call you at work if they know that your employer disapproves
- Say that they will garnish, seize, attach, or sell your property unless they intend to legally do so
- Give false credit information about you
- Say that actions will be taken against you that cannot legally be taken
- Take or threaten to take your property unless this can legally be done
- Collect any amount greater than your debt unless allowed by law
- Deposit a postdated check before the date on the check
- Send correspondence that resembles official court or government documents
- Use threats of harm to a person, property, or a person's reputation
- Use a false name

The three things collectors *can* do:
- Identify themselves and the name of their company
- Tell you why they are calling, the amount you owe, the account, and the creditor's name
- Send you a letter within 5 business days after they first contact you, giving you the creditor's name, how much is owed, and instructions to follow if the information is incorrect

Debt collectors can incur steep penalties (fines and restrictions) if they do not abide by the law. If you feel that a debt collector has broken the Fair Debt Collection Practices Act, report this activity to your state attorney general's office. For further information regarding the

Fair Debt Collection Practices Act, you can contact the Federal Trade Commission (FTC) office in your state. Ask for the department that handles debt collection and consumer protection issues, then file a complaint.

Step 5: How to Negotiate with Creditors or Collectors
When negotiating with creditors or collectors, remember to consider what is available in your budget after you have done what you can to cut costs and/or increase income. Speak with a manager if possible. Get whatever was agreed to in writing. Make sure creditors agree in writing to remove all derogatory information from your credit history with all three credit reporting agencies. They will most likely change your rating from I-9 or R-9 (or whatever it may be) to 0. Zero means no rating, which is better than a bad rating.

1. Ask if you can make lower monthly payments for a few months until you get your finances together.

2. Ask if they can extend the length of your loan period to reduce monthly payments.

3. Ask if you can go without making payments for 30, 60, or 90 days (especially in auto repossession situations).

4. For charged-off accounts, offer the collection agency 25% of the original balance owed. Some will accept this offer, while others will try to get more. However, you must remember that the creditor that transferred this account to the collection agency has already written this debt off and does not expect to collect from you. The creditor has already received a tax deduction for this bad debt. Anything the creditor collects is extra profit. For settlement amounts less than the original amount owed, collection agencies will usually ask for payment in full. For example, if you offer to pay $250 of a $1,000 bill, they will want you to pay the full $250 instead of making monthly payments. Sometimes, they will give you the chance to pay this amount off in two or three installments if you are persistent.

Step 6: How to Clear Up Your Credit History
There are three main credit bureaus (credit reporting agencies) that keep a record of your financial activities as far as credit usage is concerned. They are Experian (formerly TRW), Trans Union, and Equifax. Clearing up your credit history with these three bureaus will take diligence and persistence.

Here are the steps that are involved:

1. Request a copy of your credit report from all three agencies at least once a year. Sometimes they have different information about you. In addition, you will want to clear up everything with each one of them. Review each report thoroughly to ensure that everything is accurate.

Equifax, Inc. P. O. Box 105873 Atlanta, Georgia 30348 (800) 685-1111 Credit Information Center	(Provides credit report for a fee) (Can order online at www.credit.equifax.com)
Experian (Formerly TRW) P. O. Box 2002 Allen, TX 75013 (888) 397-3742	(Provides credit report for a fee) (Can order online at www.creditexpert.com)
Trans Union Information P. O. Box 1000 Chesterfield, PA (800) 888-4213 Consumer Relations	(Provides credit report for a fee)

NOTE: If you have been denied credit, employment, or insurance within the last 60 days or have experienced adverse action (negative change in your credit limit), been a victim of fraud, or are unemployed, your credit report can be ordered for *free*.

2. Write to the credit bureau if you find inaccurate information on your credit report. Because credit bureaus handle so much information, they can make mistakes, especially if you have a common name. Make sure that your Social Security number is correct and that the correct creditors are listed. Check each account balance and status.

3. Delinquent accounts cannot be kept on your report for more than 7 years from the time of your last transaction, according to the Fair Credit Reporting Act. Transactions consist of payments or purchases made by the consumer, not adjustments or status changes made by the creditor.

NOTE: The exception to this rule is bankruptcy, which remains on the credit report for up to 10 years.

4. According to the law, you can dispute the accuracy of any information on your credit report with the credit bureau. The bureau must follow up with the creditor to verify this information. If the creditor does not dispute your claim within a reasonable period of time (usually 30 days), the credit reporting agency must remove the derogatory information from your report. Because of the large volume of information that creditors and collectors handle on a daily basis, very few take the time to verify questionable information, which usually results in this information being removed from your credit history.

NOTE: This action does not relieve you of your responsibility to pay off this debt.

Understanding Your Credit Rating

Every detail of when we pay, how much we pay, and when we finally pay our debts off is being watched and recorded as if we're playing in a televised football game, only the game we are playing is the game of life, and the football is our credit. Complex statistics are being calculated all the time to determine our credit rating, with R-1 being the best rating and R-9 the worst rating.

The following list shows you what the credit ratings on your report mean.

R stands for **revolving credit** and **I** stands for **installment credit.** For example, R-1 or I-1 means that for these accounts you have excellent credit, R-5 or I-5 means that you are 120 days past due on these accounts, and R-9 or I-9 means that these accounts have been charged off.

0 - Too new to rate
1 - Current
2 - 30 days past the due date
3 - 60 days past the due date
4 - 90 days past the due date
5 - 120 days past the due date
6 - 150 days past the due date
7 - 180 days past the due date
[-] No history reported for that month
[Blank] No history maintained

Step 7: How to Avoid Bankruptcy or Recover If You Have Already Filed

Bankruptcy has been a hot ticket for many individuals who have sought to clear up their financial problems. They believed that it was a safe and easy way to get back on their feet fiscally. However, the truth about bankruptcy is that it is a major strike against your credit history and a substantial blow to your financial future. It is such a major problem that the federal government has enacted legislation deterring consumers from filing. Here is the lowdown on what bankruptcy actually does, which is something you won't see in the multitude of TV commercials that encourage you to file bankruptcy.

Chapter 7 Bankruptcy (Liquidation Bankruptcy)

With a Chapter 7 bankruptcy, your personal assets are sold to pay off your debts. Any remaining debts will be discharged if you do not have enough to cover everything. You are able to keep some of your personal assets, such as your home, car, and furniture. Meanwhile, there are major obligations that you are not able to discharge (pay). These include federal income taxes owed, alimony, and child support payments. A Chapter 7 bankruptcy stays on your credit report for 7 years and makes it virtually impossible for you to apply for credit for a full 10-year period. This option also decreases the chance that you will achieve your financial goals. You may no longer owe creditors, but you will be broke. There will be no money or other assets to use for emergencies. Instead of choosing this option, you can sell off the personal assets of your choice. Or better yet, try some of the debt-reduction strategies we covered earlier.

Chapter 13 Bankruptcy (Wage Earner Bankruptcy)
A Chapter 13 bankruptcy allows you to reorganize by setting up a payment plan to fit your budget. Under the supervision of the bankruptcy court, you repay your creditors. The court acts as trustee, giving you 3 to 5 years to repay them. Additionally, the court may allow you to discount your debt, meaning that you will repay only a percentage of every dollar you owe. No assets will be sold to repay the debt. Within 1 day of filing, a restraining order will be sent to all of your creditors to stop legal action against you and to stop the seizure of your assets. This action also puts a stop to collector's calls and halts the accumulation of all interest, penalties, and fees. A hearing is scheduled to work out your payment plan. You can even file the paperwork on your own for both a Chapter 13 and a Chapter 7 bankruptcy with the court (no legal advice will be provided).

A Chapter 13 bankruptcy is not as detrimental as a Chapter 7 bankruptcy and stays on your credit report for 7 years. Some individuals have still been able to get loans after a couple of years with a Chapter 13 arrangement. What many do not realize, however, is that, under this provision, your entire paycheck will be sent to the bankruptcy trustee to pay your creditors first, then the "leftovers" will go to you. You will have no control over your paycheck until every debt is paid. This, of course, must involve your employer. Why do this when you can set up your own payment arrangement with creditors who are more than eager to cut a deal? You could save yourself embarrassment with your employer, continue to control your own money, and avoid derogatory remarks on your credit report. I bet they won't tell you *that* on the TV commercials!

NOTE: When considering bankruptcy, one should always ask, "Why pay someone to do for me what I can do for myself for free?" You would be surprised what payment arrangements or payoff agreements creditors are willing to accept if you will just be committed and persistent.

If you have already filed bankruptcy, here are a few things you can do to better the situation:

- When you get back on your feet financially, get the bankruptcy discharged as soon as possible by paying off debts sooner.
- Accelerate the payments by sending additional money to creditors whenever possible.
- When you are able, set up additional savings to pay off your creditors sooner.

- Use some of the strategies covered earlier in this chapter to pay down debts faster, e.g., increase hours on the job, take on part-time work, start an inexpensive small business to generate extra income, or seek help from family or friends if possible.

Step 8: How to Get Free Professional Advice

There are several ways to get free professional advice. You can call the **Consumer Credit Counseling Service (CCCS)** to set up an appointment with a certified professional counselor to help you negotiate with creditors and get out of debt. Your counselor will set up a debt management program for you. CCCS sets up this program in conjunction with the creditor to help the consumer maintain set payment amounts. CCCS will also help consumers develop a budget to stay on track and avoid problems in the future. One must set and keep appointments during specific times of the day, which may not be convenient for all consumers. Consumers can also call CCCS' sister program, **Money Management International (MMI)**, to receive assistance from a certified professional counselor. Because consumers' work schedules may make it difficult for them to keep their appointments with CCCS, MMI was developed to meet the needs of those who require more flexibility. MMI counselors are available 24 hours a day, 7 days a week. You can meet with them by phone, e-mail, regular mail, or in person.

How do these organizations provide such useful services for free? They are nonprofit organizations that are financially supported by creditors. This creates a win-win situation. Consumers get back on track with their finances with professional counseling at no charge, CCCS and MMI get paid for providing a much-needed service that is free to consumers, and creditors receive consistent payments on accounts that could have remained delinquent for years or that may have been charged off.

The organizations can be contacted as indicated below.

Consumer Credit Counseling Service (800) 873-CCCS (2227), or check your directory for the nearest location	**Money Management International** (800) 762-2271 www.MMINTL.org

Lastly, there is **Debtors Anonymous**, a program similar to Alcoholics Anonymous. Debtors Anonymous is a global organization founded in 1976 with the mission of helping individuals get and remain debt free. They help individuals through group meetings in local churches and public facilities. Contact the general office in Massachusetts at (781) 453-2743, check your telephone directory or on the web at www.DebtorsAnonymous.org for a local meeting place. The services are free.

Summary

We have covered a great deal of helpful information in this chapter. By following the eight steps to credit freedom, many will lay the groundwork for tremendous financial gains in their lives, with their families, in their churches, on their jobs, and in their communities. I trust that this chapter has made a significant impact on how you move forward in your financial life. The end of this chapter includes five sample letters and a summary of the procedure you can use when contacting credit information bureaus.

You can also use these types of letters to request that incorrect identifying information be removed from your credit history, such as mistakes related to your name, current employer, Social Security number, address, etc. You can also use these letters to have unauthorized inquiries removed from your credit report.

NOTE: Always check with the credit bureau before sending any letters to make sure you have an accurate address, telephone number, and procedures.

Questions

1. What three things did Proverbs 22 identify to help us prioritize our general and financial behavior?

2. What were the three suggestions for using credit wisely and keeping your credit report clear?

3. Explain three of the six ways to control compulsive spending.

4. What are some of the various ways one can pay off debts, and what are the pitfalls one should avoid when using these strategies?

5. How can consumers stop receiving aggravating calls from credit collectors?

6. Name five things creditors cannot legally do to consumers.

7. What three things must creditors do when contacting a consumer?

8. What four strategies can be used to negotiate with creditors?

9. What four things can a person do to clear up derogatory information on his or her credit report?

10. Name the three credit reporting bureaus.

11. What is the best way to avoid bankruptcy?

12. What should one do if he or she has already filed bankruptcy?

13. What agencies provide free counseling for people with debt problems?

The next few pages will cover the procedure and sample letters you can use when contacting credit bureaus.

Procedure for Contacting Credit Bureaus
1. Write a letter to all three credit bureaus requesting a copy of your credit report.
2. After receiving a copy of your report, review it for incorrect information and send the appropriate letter(s) to correct the problem.
3. Identify all of the correct derogatory remarks on your report, and use the strategies covered in this chapter to remove them.

Sample # 1   To Request A Copy Of Your Credit Report

Credit Bureau Name										Date
Consumer Relations Department
Street Address
City, State, Zip

Dear Credit Administrator:

Please send a copy of my credit report.

Your name: last, first, middle initial
Generation: (Jr., III, etc.)
Spouse's first name
Current address
Previous address
Year of birth
Social Security number

I have included a recent copy of my utility bill to verify my address. I would appreciate your immediate assistance in this matter.

Sincerely,

(Your signature)

Please send to:		Name
					Address
					City, State, Zip

Sample # 2 To Request A Copy Of Your Credit Report Following Credit Denial

Credit Bureau Name   Date
Consumer Relations Department
Street Address
City, State, Zip

Dear Credit Administrator:

I was denied credit on (date) by (name of creditor) because of information on my credit report. Please send a copy of my credit report.

Your name: last, first, middle initial
Generation: (Jr., III, etc.)
Spouse's first name
Current address
Previous address
Year of birth
Social Security number

I would appreciate your immediate assistance in this matter.

Sincerely,

(Your signature)

Please send to: Name
                        Address
                        City, State, Zip

SAMPLE #3   To Dispute Accounts On Your Credit Report

Credit Bureau Name   Date
Consumer Relations Department
Address
City, State, Zip

Dear Credit Administrator:

In reviewing my credit report, I discovered accounts that are inaccurate. I am requesting that the following accounts be investigated and verified:

Creditor's name:
Creditor (subscriber) code:
Account number:
Reason for dispute:
* (You can include more than one account on this letter)

I understand that according to the Fair Credit Reporting Act (Section 611), the above request will be investigated and I will be notified of your results within thirty (30) days. Please send an updated copy of my credit report when you complete your investigation.

Your name: last, first, middle initial
Generation: (Jr., III, etc.)
Spouse's first name:
Current address:
Previous address:
Year of birth:
Social Security number:

I would appreciate your immediate assistance in this matter.

Sincerely,

(Your signature)

Please send to: Name
                  Address
                  City, State, Zip

The Urban Guide to Biblical Money Management | 69

Sample #4   To Request Removal Of Credit Information Older Than 7 Years

Credit Bureau Name   Date
Consumer Relations Department
Address
City, State, Zip

Dear Credit Administrator:

I have recently received a copy of my credit report. The following account(s) have had no transactions for seven years or more.

Creditor name:
Creditor (Subscriber) code:
Account number:
* (You can include more than one account on this letter)

My credit report shows a derogatory remark on this account. Under the Fair Credit Reporting Act (Sections 605-607), the statute of limitations has expired, and this account should be deleted from my credit report. Please delete the following account(s) and send an updated copy of my report.

Your name: last, first, middle initial
Generation: (Jr., III, etc.)
Spouse's first name:
Current address:
Previous address:
Year of birth:
Social Security number

I would appreciate your immediate assistance in this matter.

Sincerely,

(Your signature)

Please send to: Name
                  Address
                  City, State, Zip

Sample # 5   To Place A Consumer Statement On Your Credit Report

Credit Bureau Name   Date
Consumer Relations Department
Address
City, State, Zip

Dear Credit Administrator:

Upon recently reviewing my credit report, I discovered an account that needs explanation and am requesting that the following consumer statement be added to my report.

Creditor name:
Creditor (subscriber) code:
Account number:
Consumer statement: _____
_____
_____
_____

* (You can include more than one account on this letter)

Your name: last, first, middle initial
Generation: (Jr., III, etc.)
Spouse's first name:
Current address:
Previous address:
Year of birth:
Social Security number:

I would appreciate your immediate assistance in this matter.

Sincerely,

(Your signature)
Please send to: Name
                  Address
                  City, State, Zip

The Urban Guide to Biblical Money Management | 71

Section III

BUILDING FOR YOUR FUTURE

Proverbs 21:20
"Precious treasure remains in the house of the wise, but the fool devours it."

Building for our tomorrows should be a consistent activity in our lives because this has a major impact on the lifestyles we are able to attain and maintain, in both the short run and the long run. If we choose a life of spending only versus one of balancing spending with saving, we will pay a handsome price, as is pointed out in the Scripture above. "Through wisdom a house is built, and by understanding it is established" (Proverbs 24:3). In other words, by increasing your knowledge and the number of knowledgeable people you come in contact with regarding financial matters, the greater your chances at building a sound financial future.

In this section, we will explore "Bank and Stock Market Investment Instruments (Online and Offline)," "Home Ownership and Investment Property Matters," and "Entrepreneurship Matters" in Chapters 5, 6, and 7, respectively. We will investigate a variety of topics, including determining how much investment risk one should assume and using investment and savings instruments to build your portfolio. We will also examine saving for education and retirement on your own and through your employer as well as investing to beat inflation. Additionally, this section will outline the benefits of home ownership versus renting, direct real estate purchase versus real estate purchase via the Internet, and how to use entrepreneurship and small business development as a financial planning tool.

Chapter 5

◆◆◆

USING BANKING AND STOCK MARKET INVESTMENT INSTRUMENTS (OFFLINE AND ONLINE)

This chapter will help you determine how much risk you are willing to assume before investing by using a Risk Tolerance Grid. The chapter will also discuss how one's personal situation (e.g., family status, job status, income, budget, assets, and debts) affects one's investments. The primary focus of the chapter will be on the types of savings and investment instruments that are available, where they rank in terms of safety versus risk, and how these investments can be used to achieve short-term, medium-term, and long-term goals, and to provide for education and retirement. Savings will be discussed, as will keys to investing through your employer savings plans and explain the basic components offered through online banking and brokerage services, and methods of investing to beat inflation.

Hosea 4:6
"My people are destroyed for lack of knowledge."

The greatest part of sound investing is getting a basic understanding of what you are putting your money into by working with a financial professional and reading on your own. Hosea 4:6 not only reveals the downside of not searching out a matter; it can also be seen as an exhortation to gather as much information as possible to avoid roadblocks that could destroy one's financial future.

How Much Investment Risk Should You Assume?
After you have paid the monthly bills, you may have disposable income left over. What you do with this disposable income after you spend a little on yourself will be determined by

your **risk tolerance**. Your risk tolerance tells you and your financial advisor how much investment risk you are willing to assume comfortably. To determine your risk tolerance, consider the Risk Tolerance Grid shown in Table 5.1.

Of the total amount of funds you have to save and invest, what percentage (%) would you prefer to invest in each category?

#1 Prefer Safest Investments (Lowest Risk/Lowest Return)	#2 Prefer Moderately Safe Investments With Little Risk (Low To Medium Risk and Return)
% of investments desired here _____	% of investments desired here _____
#3 Occasional Risk (Medium To High Risk and Return)	#4 Earn The Highest Return Possible No Matter What The Risk (Highest Risk and Return)
% of investments desired here _____	% of investments desired here _____

Table 5.1 • **Risk Tolerance Grid**

#1 Prefer Safest Investments (Lowest Risk/Lowest Return)	#2 Prefer Moderately Safe Investments With Little Risk (Low To Medium Risk and Return)
-Checking Account -Savings Account -Money Market Account/Fund -Certificate of Deposit (CD) -Treasury Bill, Note, Bond -U.S. Savings Bonds	-Utility Stocks and Mutual Funds -High-Grade Corporate Bonds -Income Mutual Funds -Blue-Chip Stocks and Mutual Funds -Mid-Cap Mutual Funds -High-Grade Municipal Bonds
#3 Occasional Risk (Medium To High Risk and Return)	**#4 Earn The Highest Return Possible No Matter What The Risk (Highest Risk and Return)**
-Small-Cap Mutual Funds/Stocks -Aggressive-Growth Mutual Funds -High-Yield Junk Bonds/Funds -Real Estate Investment Trust (REIT) -Real Estate	-Options -Futures -Gold/Precious Metals -Collectibles

Table 5.2 • Risk Tolerance Grid Investment Categories

Let's look at the savings and investments that would fall into each of the four categories on the Risk Tolerance Grid in Table 5.2.

Individuals who put their money in **category #1** seek income. They want regular dividends or interest and/or a specified rate of return.

Individuals who put their money in **category #2** seek income and capital appreciation. They want moderate income (interest or dividends) and an increase in the value of the underlying investment, which they would recognize through the sale or exchange of the investment.

Individuals who place their income in **category #3** will take above-average risks to get above-average returns. They will forgo income to achieve high growth in the value of the underlying investment.

Individuals who place their money in **category #4** are the high rollers who will invest for the purpose of receiving extremely high returns on their investment. They will run the risk of losing their entire investment in a very short period of time (seconds, minutes, hours, days, etc.) for megareturns. They also use this category to hedge (insure) their other investments.

As we review the Risk Tolerance Grid, we should take the opportunity to evaluate where we want to put our money. It would be easier, however, if we knew which savings and investment instruments fit into each category.

NOTE: Generally, the younger you are, the more risk you can take; the older you are, the less risk you can take.

How Your Personal Situation Affects How You Invest
Whenever you have funds to invest, whether it's money left over after the bills are paid, money received from a retirement plan when you left your last job, money you inherited, money received as a gift, money you were awarded in a legal settlement, etc., you must do this exercise. After determining how much risk you are willing to assume, you must consider your personal situation. This would include reviewing your family status. How many dependents do you have? Is there just one, or are there children and/or a spouse? Should the money be used for education or retirement savings? You also need to review your job status. Are you expecting a substantial salary increase, or should you consider investing in your own business? Your income status should also be reviewed. Is your income so great that you need to look for tax-sheltered investments, or is it so low that you need to invest to receive additional income today as well as save for retirement? You definitely must review your budget. Do you need additional money to pay down some debts, take a vacation, remodel your home, etc.?

Use a little money to reward yourself and invest the rest in your goals.

After thoroughly reviewing your personal situation, you are ready to start looking at savings and investment options. Make sure you keep your financial goals in mind. Many people skip this fiscal exercise and end up spending all the additional money they receive in investment earnings. A good number of people will not even be able to remember exactly how they spent the money. One suggestion is to use a little money to reward yourself and invest the rest in your goals. This strategy would benefit you in both the long run and the short run. However, all retirement savings should be reinvested or rolled over to avoid tax penalties.

Types of Banking and Stock Market Investment Instruments and the Risks/Rewards Associated with Them

1. Checking Account
A checking account is designed for multiple transactions. It has an indefinite term, and account holders can withdraw and deposit as many times as they wish. Some checking accounts carry minimum balances and fees for ATM withdrawals, check writing, and, sometimes teller transactions. Some checking accounts pay inerest, while others do not. Interest paid is usually lower than on savings and money market acounts. Checking accounts are insured by the Federal Deposit Insurance Corporation (FDIC) or the National Credit Union Association (NCUA) for amounts up to $100,000 and are virtually risk free.

2. Savings Account

A savings account is a no-risk account that can be established with a financial institution (usually a bank or credit union) for an indefinite period of time. A savings account is insured up to $100,000 by the FDIC or NCUA and pays lower interest rates than most other investments. It has unrestricted deposits and withdrawals.

3. Money Market Account/Fund

A money market account or fund is a no-risk account that has no regulated minimum term and allows a limited number of checks to be written per month. It generally has a higher balance and higher interest than a savings or checking account. Money market accounts are insured by the FDIC or NCUA. Money market funds are similar but are offered through brokerage companies. They are not FDIC-inured, but are virtually risk free and offer limited check-writing privileges as well. Many investors use their money market account as a "sweep account" in which to hold funds that a broker uses to buy stocks and other investments for them. Extra income and dividends are "swept" (deposited) back into this account.

4. Certificate of Deposit (CD)

A certificate of deposit (CD) is a type of savings account with a fixed minimum term, initial deposit, and interest rate. The rate remains the same throughout the term. There is generally a penalty for premature withdrawals. CD's can usually be purchased for time frames ranging from 1 month to 10 years. At some financial institutions, variable-rate CD's are offered. The interest rate is tied to some financial index and moves as the index moves. Fixed-rate CD's are insured by the FDIC or NCUA.

5. Treasury Bills and Notes

Treasury bills (T-bills) are short-term obligations of the U.S. government with maturities not exceeding 1 year. T-bills do not have a stated interest rate. They are traded at a discount from their face value. The return to the investor is the difference between the discounted price and the par value (the price at which the T-bill matures). T-bills are virtualy risk free if held until they mature. They are available for terms of 3 months, 6 months, and 1 year. The minimum investment is $10,000, with multiples of $5,000 thereafter.

Treasury notes are intermediate obligations of the U.S. government with maturities that range between 1 and 10 years. T-notes are not discounted like T-bills. They pay a fixed rate of interest twice a year with coupons. The investment amount can be in denominations of $1,000 or $5,000. All treasury securities are backed by the full faith and credit of the U.S. government.

6. U.S. Savings Bonds

A U.S. savings bond is a savings certificate offered by the U.S. government to individual investors in small amounts. Bonds can be purchased in denominations of $50, $75, $100, $200, $500, $1,000, $5,000, and $10,000. The annual purchase limit is $30,000. These bonds are sold at a 50% discount (e.g., a $50 bond would cost you $25) and can earn tax-deferred interest for up to 30 years. The interest on the bond is lower than that on most investments and is not known until the bond is redeemed. These bonds are also backed by the full faith and credit of the U.S. government.

7. Stocks

Stocks are securities that represent ownership interest in a corporation. Purchasing stock gives individuals the chance to own part of a corporation. Stocks may or may not pay dividend income depending on how well the company does, and stock value may increase or decrease based on the company's performance. These investments may be sold at any time and have no insurance or backing. Despite the crashes in the stock market and the periodic fluctuations, stock has outperformed every other investment since the inception of the stock market. Stock objectives can be evaluated in three categories: income, growth and income, and aggressive growth.

Income stocks provide investors with consistent dividends from safer companies (blue-chip and utility companies) that have been in business for a good while, e.g., McDonald's, IBM, Com Ed, Ameritech, and Sears. While companies in this income category generally provide consistent dividends, they do not offer much opportunity for growth or increase in price per share.

Growth and income (total return) stocks provide some dividend payment and the opportunity for capital appreciation (increase in stock price and in investment value). If you want the best of both worlds, an investment in growth and income stocks may be for you. Because you have the opportunity to realize both investment growth and income, you generally will have to settle for a lower rate of dividends than most income stocks would pay and a lower growth rate than most aggressive-growth stocks could achieve. Stocks in this category are offered by large to mid-sized companies. Growth and dividends are not guaranteed.

Growth and aggressive-growth stocks have historically provided the most opportunity for high return on investment, even though growth is not guaranteed. This type of stock investment is not for the faint of heart but for those interested in risking their money to earn a greater return than possible with income or total return stocks. The companies in this category are generally smaller, unknown entities.

Initial Public Offerings (IPOs)

As the name implies, initial public offerings are stocks made available by companies that are going public for the first time. These companies have made the transition from being privately held (privately funded by owners) to receiving funding from the general public. IPOs make it possible for individuals to buy stock in companies that trade on a stock exchange such as the New York Stock Exchange, American Stock Exchange (AMEX), or National Association of Securities Dealers Automatic Quotation System. While this is a good way for investors to get in at the ground level of a company's growth and reap astronomical profits, one must be aware that some IPOs may not do well. Many investors lose their money on

IPO investments; since there isn't much research available showing historical performance, it's a gamble. Here's a tip on reducing your risk when investing in IPOs: As with other riskier investments, one should limit the amount of money invested to test the waters; and, of course, do not use money designated for other budgetary items.

Direct Public Offerings (DPOs)
With direct public offerings, companies forgo the traditional path followed by IPO issuers. DPOs are sold directly to the public from the corporation. Because DPOs are not subject to the regulation that IPOs are subject to, they involve a greater degree of risk to investors. Individual investors are responsible for conducting their own research into the company. DPO investments are designed for the sophisticated investor who has timely access to market information. They are offered through the Internet (try www.witcapital.com).

Evaluating and Selecting Good Stocks
To evaluate stocks, investors can read the *Value Line Investment Survey*, which provides safety ratings and financial information for 1,700 stocks, or review *Standard and Poor's Stock Reports*. Both are available in most libraries. There are other strategies that investors can use to evaluate stocks as well:

- Review the **earnings per share.** If earnings increase every year, the company is doing well.

- Check the **P/E (price to earnings) ratio**. This ratio tells whether a stock is overpriced or perhaps underpriced and is the single most widely used evaluation tool because it reflects investors' opinions of stocks in comparison to the stock market as a whole. The P/E ratio compares the company's current stock price per share to its net income or earnings per share. Companies with higher P/E ratios could be heading for a fall in the price of their stock. Companies with lower P/E ratios are the best companies to add to your portfolio because they are generally headed for a price increase.

- Research the company's **book value**. The book value shows the difference between the company's assets and liabilities (debts). A low book value reflects too much debt, while a high book value shows low debts and good opportunity for investment growth.

These evaluation tools can be found in *The Wall Street Journal, Value Line Investment Survey, Standard and Poor's Stock Reports, Investor's Business Daily,* etc.

Before investing in stocks:

- Look for larger companies with a good track record of stable growth, debts, and profits.
- Invest for the long term, i.e., 5 years or more.
- Diversify your investment dollars in various stocks, using the Risk Tolerance Grid (Table 5.1) to help you.
- Get advice from a qualified investment professional.

8. Bonds

Corporate bonds are interest-bearing certificates of indebtedness issued by corporations. With bonds, companies are borrowing money from investors with a promise to pay a steady stream of income in equal installments every 6 months. If the company does not default, you will receive all of your principal (initial investment) at maturity (the end of the bond's term). If you must sell your bond before the maturity date, it may be worth more or less than what you paid for it. Bond values fluctuate with interest rates. The price an investor pays for a bond will decrease if interest rates in the market go up. If interest rates go down, the price of the bond will go up.

Keep in mind, however, that if you do not sell your bond before maturity, rate fluctuations will not change the value of your principal or the rate of interest. Generally, corporate bonds pay a higher rate than government bonds because of the higher risk of the company defaulting. The less financial stability a company has, the greater the risk. Companies compensate willing investors by paying them a higher interest rate. Corporate bonds come in $1,000 denominations and in some cases may be available only in blocks (e.g., five for $5,000).

These bonds provide three types of yields: coupon rate, current yield, and yield to maturity. The **coupon rate** is the fixed annual stated interest rate paid on a bond. For example, a $1,000 bond with an interest rate of 10% will pay $100 per year or $50 twice a year. The **current yield** is the percentage of income received annually on a bond. For example, corporate bonds usually sell at a discount from the face value stated on the bond. You may pay $900 for a bond that will be worth $1,000 at some specified date in the future. The difference between $1,000 and $900 is $100. To calculate the current yield, divide $100 by $900 and multiply that amount by 100. In this example, the current yield is 11.1%. The **yield to maturity** takes into account the annual yield paid from the time of initial investment to the time of maturity. The yield to maturity on a 5-year bond paying 10% interest for which the investor pays $900 is 13%. You can ask your financial advisor to calculate the yields for you.

Municipal bonds are long-term, tax-exempt securities that represent a loan to state and local governments and their agencies. Generally, no federal income taxes are paid on these investments. State bonds are tax exempt for investors who live in the state where the bonds are issued. City bonds are also tax exempt where this residency rule applies. State and city municipal bonds are used to finance building projects such as bridges, stadiums, public housing, road improvements, etc. Municipal bonds are more useful to investors in higher income tax brackets—for example, those in a 28%, 31%, or higher tax bracket. For example, if the tax-exempt interest is 7%, this is equivalent to a 9.72% yield for someone in the 28% tax bracket (7% / 1.28 = 9.72%) or a 10.14% yield for someone in the 31% tax bracket (7% / 1.31 = 10.14%). Municipal bonds come in denominations of $1,000 with a typical minimum purchase of a block of five for $5,000. These bonds are longer-term investments with maturities from 5 to 30 years.

There are two main categories of municipal bonds: general obligation bonds and revenue bonds. **General obligation bonds** are backed by the state or city taxing authority from which they were issued and are generally safer than revenue bonds. **Revenue bonds** are backed by the specific project or agency which they are used to finance; for example, New York State Thruway or Illinois State Tollway revenue bonds are repaid by fees collected at toll booths in the respective states. Revenue bonds have longer terms than general obligation bonds because they carry greater risk.

Rating Bonds

Bonds are rated by the Moody's and Standard and Poor's 500 (S & P 500) rating services (Table 5.3). These services research the financial condition of the bond issuers, the state of the economy, and how well companies in the same business are doing. Their primary goal is to inform investors of risks associated with bond issues. Both services rank corporate, municipal, and international bonds. Treasury bonds are not ranked because they are backed by the full faith and credit of the U.S. government, which can raise taxes to pay off debts if it needs to.

As an investor, you should review the difference between investment grade bonds and junk bonds. Investment grade bonds are any bonds rated Baa or higher by Moody's and BBB or higher by Standard and Poor's. Everything else is considered a junk bond. Junk bonds carry high risk and promise high returns. With junk bonds, there is a good chance that the issuer will not repay its debt. However, some investors are willing to take the risk because the yields are so high.

Zero coupon bonds are a form of fixed-income debt that owe their name to the fact that they do not bear coupons that can be redeemed for interest. Instead, the zero coupon bond is sold at a deep discount to investors who receive nothing until the maturity date. The return received at maturity is the difference between the price at which the bond was purchased and the price when redeemed. The maturity date varies anywhere from 6 months to 24 years or more (usually 7 10 years). The minimum investment can be anywhere from $1,000 to $1,000,000. Different types of zero coupon bonds are available through corporations, municipal agencies, and brokerage companies. The yield, liquidity (ability to convert into cash), risk, and other factors vary.

S & P	Moody's	Explanation
AAA	Aaa	Best-quality bonds with smallest degree of risk. Issuers are highly stable.
AA	Aa	High quality with slight long-term risk.
A	A	High to medium quality with good potential but vulnerable to changes in the economy.
BBB	Baa	Medium quality with adequate potential but do not provide long-term reliability.
BB	Ba	Provide some security, yet speculative.
B	B	Can pay interest now, yet carry the risk of future default.
CCC	Caa	Poor quality with definite danger of default.
CC	Ca	Highly speculative and often in default.
C	C	Lowest rating with very poor prospects of continued repayment.
D	–	In default.

Table 5.3 • Bond Rating Chart

9. Mutual Funds

Mutual funds pool investors' money together to purchase a variety of investments, including stocks, bonds, and money market instruments. The mutual fund is set up as a portfolio and managed by a professional portfolio manager. As with stocks, mutual fund prices are represented by **net asset value** versus price per share. As the net asset value fluctuates, the value of your investment fluctuates. Mutual funds are set up based on investment objectives set by portfolio managers. Mutual funds can pay dividends, provide an increase in the initial investment, and provide capital gains distribution when securities are sold for a profit inside the fund.

Mutual funds provide various advantages in comparison with other investments:

- They are a safer investment because of the diversified portfolio of various investments.
- The mutual fund company researches the individual securities that make up the portfolio. Mutual funds also offer various investment objectives to suit different investors.

- They require a smaller minimum investment. For example, $25 can be automatically debited from one's bank account. Some funds will accept a minimum investment as little as $250.
- They provide high liquidity; that is, they allow the investor to sell shares and redeem them for cash very easily and in a short period of time (1 business day).
- They offer flexibility. Dividends can be automatically reinvested back into the fund or paid out to the investor. Also, it is very easy to switch between funds in the family of funds provided by the mutual fund company.

Investment objectives drive the kinds of investments that are selected for a mutual fund portfolio. The investment objectives also determine the degree of risk the fund will assume. Let's look at the different investment objectives that a mutual fund portfolio can have.

Types of Mutual Funds

Income funds are more conservative investments that seek to provide current income by investing in a mix of bonds, high-yielding common stocks, and preferred stock.

Balanced funds are made up of bonds and preferred stock from major companies. They focus on long-term growth while minimizing risk to the investor.

Total return funds seek a combination of dividend income and capital appreciation (growth). They are also suitable for long-term investors.

Growth funds seek long-term growth by investing in companies with values that increase faster than inflation.

Aggressive-growth funds are the riskiest type of fund. These funds invest in speculative, small growth company stocks in developing industries.

Growth and income funds seek to provide long-term growth and current income. They invest in companies that have a solid history of paying dividends, with growth potential.

Sector funds focus on investments in a specific industry such as biotechnology or oil. Greater risk is assumed because the investments are not as diversified as those in other mutual funds.

Bond funds use a variety of bonds to make up the portfolio. They exist in four categories: high-quality, taxable, non-taxable, and high-yield. High-yield funds assume the greatest degree of risk because they invest in junk bonds.

International and global funds. International funds invest in stocks that are traded on foreign exchanges. Global funds include international and U.S. stocks.

> *"One must be very cautious when investing in funds with back-end fees. If your investment is constantly growing, this will be the most expensive mutual fund choice."*

Money market funds invest in a variety of IOUs issued by the government and corporations. A money market fund generally pays a couple of percentage points above bank savings accounts. A money market account usually allows check-writing privileges and can also act as a sweep account for dividends or interest from other investments. A money market fund is a safe investment. It can also be obtained in tax-exempt form.

Social funds invest in companies that incorporate various social and/or cultural objectives in their day-to-day business activities (e.g., eliminating animal testing, refusing products made through forced labor in third world countries, partnering with African-American-owned companies, etc.).

While mutual funds provide an easy, less expensive way for small investors to tap into the stock market and bond market, get sound market research, and obtain professional portfolio management, they are not risk free. Investors can reduce risk by dollar cost averaging as well as by investing in a variety of funds (if possible) and investing for the long run. Dollar cost averaging involves investing a fixed amount on a periodic basis (e.g., every pay period, monthly, quarterly). Because the mutual fund will fluctuate with the stock market, you get the advantage of receiving the average price when price per share goes up or down, if you invest over the long run. Other things you can do to reduce your risk include studying publications that evaluate the funds (e.g., *Money Magazine* or *Kiplinger's Personal Finance*) or reading the fund prospectus before investing. A prospectus gives investors the details of the investments in the portfolio and other pertinent information. You can request the prospectus from the company or your broker.

Mutual Fund Fees

- **No-load** mutual funds do not require a fee for individuals to invest. This means that when you invest $1,000, the entire $1,000 will be invested.
- **Low-load** mutual funds require a minimum fee when one invests (e.g., 1%—3%).
- **Fully loaded** mutual funds charge fees between 4% and 8.5%.
- **Front-end** fees are paid each time the investor makes an initial purchase of mutual fund shares. For example: if the fee is 5% and an individual invests $1,000, 5% or $50 (.05 $1,000) will be taken out first, while the remaining $950 ($1,000 $50) will be invested in the fund.
- **Back-end** fees are charged when investors withdraw their money from a mutual fund. For example, when you invest $1,000, the entire amount is invested in the fund. Let's say your account grows to $2,000 and you now want to withdraw it. If the fee is 6%, you will pay $120 (.06 $2,000) to withdraw your money, leaving you with $1,780 ($2,000—$120).

One must be very cautious when investing in funds with back-end fees. If your investment is constantly growing, this will be the most expensive mutual fund choice. Since there is no limit to how much your fund could grow, there is also no limit to how much you may have to pay in commission fees. Some back-end-loaded funds have instituted a declining fee schedule: the longer an investor's money stays in the mutual fund, the lower the back-end fee becomes. The fee decreases each year until it eventually becomes zero.

- **Expense ratios** are listed in financial publications. This ratio reflects operating, management, administrative, and 12-b1 (services and distribution) fees. These fees are reflected in the net asset value or the per-share price of a mutual fund. The expense ratio will be higher for some funds to compensate for no-load to low-load fee schedules. The higher the expense ratio, the lower the net asset value of the fund.

10. Real Estate Investment Trusts (REIT's)

A REIT is a form of indirect real estate investing. It is an unincorporated association that pools the money of many small investors who purchase certificates of ownership, much like with a mutual fund. The money is invested in real estate ventures such as mortgages (through mortgage trusts) or real property (through equity trusts). More specifically, the pool contains mortgages or income-producing properties such as apartment houses or condos, shopping centers, office buildings, and warehouses. The trust is managed by one or more trustees, and transferable shares or certificates are held by at least 100 investors. REIT's are traded on the open market like common stock. Real estate investment trusts invest in more than one property or mortgage loan to spread out the risk. REIT's pay dividends and can sell shares at a profit.

REIT's pass on most of their earnings to investors, which is why they are attractive to investors seeking high yields (high dividends) and potential profits if share prices rise. However, mortgage REIT's, which provide mortgages and construction loans, have historically paid more than equity REIT's, which own income-producing property. Mortgage REIT's are riskier than equity REIT's, especially during times when interest rates are volatile. Both pay high dividends. When considering this investment vehicle, ask your broker or investment advisor for dividend histories, investment mix, and current appraisals of properties in the portfolio.

11. Real Estate

Real estate consists of land (and the structures built on it) that is purchased for personal use or income. Real estate comes in a variety of options: single-family homes, condominiums, apartment buildings, etc. Real estate is usually a long-term investment that one should first research thoroughly. (We will cover real estate in more detail in Chapter 6.)

12. Options

An option is a contract that permits the person holding it to buy a given number of shares (usually 100) of a specific security (stock) at a specific price before a specific expiration date. The option may or may not be exercised, depending on the stock's profitability. An option that gives investors the right to buy a security is a **call option.** The right to sell is a

put option. Options can be used to **hedge** (protect current investments) or **speculate** (gamble on the market). Options allow investors to bet that the stock or other securities covered by the option will go up or down. Options mature in 3 to 9 months and are traded at an extremely high risk in extremely volatile markets. Investors can achieve enormous profits within a matter of seconds or minutes but may also experience enormous losses within the same period of time.

Before individuals are allowed to invest in options, they must pass a suitability test. Investors must prove their in-depth knowledge of the options markets and their financial ability to cover such high-risk investments. Brokers require a minimum investment of $2,500 $10,000 to get started; however, your options account could require much greater amounts of money once you start trading. Options can be purchased on stocks, stock indexes (**Dow Jones Industrial Average** [DJIA], **Standard and Poor's 500** [S & P 500], etc.), currencies (U.S. dollar, British pound, Japanese yen, etc.), interest rates (bonds issued by the U S. government, municipalities, or foreign countries), and futures contracts.

Leverage attracts investors to the options market. For very little money, one can control a large amount of capital. For example: purchasing one option allows control of 100 shares of stock; hence, 10 options would allow control of 1,000 shares of stock. Let's say the investor buys 10 call options at $75 per option. Ten options times $75 equals $750, which is the amount the investor actually pays. At the time of purchase, the stock was worth $60 per share and the 10 options carried a value of $60,000 (1,000 x $60). Then the stock price goes up by $10 dollars—$5 above a $65 strike price (the price that the investor bets the stock will rise above). The investor trades the option while the stock is at $70 for $70,000 ($70 x 1,000 shares). The profit is $5,000 ($70,000— $65,000). The return on the initial investment of $750 is ($5,000 / $750 x 100%) = 667%. This means that the investor's money grew over six times. These transactions could have taken place within an hour, several days or weeks, or a few months—very short-term. Wow! If you can make profits like that in such a short period of time, why work? Just sell your house and move to the Caribbean. Well, hold on. What if the price did not go up to $70, but instead stopped at $65? Depending on the kind of option the investor has, he or she could lose the $750 initial investment or be forced to buy 1,000 shares of stock at $65 per share. Cancel your plans for the Caribbean and come back down to earth. Options are not a game for the average investor. They are for savvy investors who can take on this high-stakes investment game. While not everyone who reads this book will be an options investor, it is important for you to know this information because someday you may be in a position to add options to your portfolio. There is also the possibility that you might be approached by an investments salesperson to purchase options, and you should know the risks involved.

13. Futures

Futures are contracts for the future delivery of a commodity at a predetermined price. Traders/investors buy and sell these contracts. In most cases, they do not take possession of the goods that the contracts represent (e.g., pork bellies, corn, wheat, orange juice, cotton, currencies, gold, CD's, T-bills, etc.). The trader/investor usually offsets the contract with an opposite transaction. Those who are expecting prices to rise buy contracts, and those expecting prices to drop sell contracts. There are about 70 types of commodities that can be traded. This is an extremely risky investment and is not designed for the average investor.

The futures game is made up of hedgers and speculators. **Hedgers** participate to protect themselves against price changes. For example: the cereal company that makes your corn flakes may want to hedge against rising corn prices because it anticipates that a heat wave will damage a large portion of the corn crop. By purchasing a contract worth several million dollars today that bets on corn prices rising at a future date, the company protects itself. When the price of corn goes up because there is less of it due to the heat wave, the value of the futures contract also increases. While the cereal maker may lose money on cereal sales at the grocery store because it had to raise the price of its cereal, it covers this loss with the profit on the futures contract.

Speculators, on the other hand, are high-rolling gamblers who invest in an effort to make large profits on price movement. Like hedgers, they do not own the underlying commodity. If speculators think wheat prices are going up, they will buy wheat futures contracts, with the understanding that they may lose their entire investment in a short period of time. The short maturity dates are set by the exchanges.

Futures contracts work much like options contracts in that they give investors very high leverage (i.e., control of a large amount of a commodity for a relatively small investment). Minimum contracts have been as low as $5,000—$10,000, but many commodity brokerage companies require high cash balances (e.g., $25,000—$50,000) to cover accounts when investments decrease in value.

14. Gold and Precious Metals

Gold and other precious metals (silver and copper) are valuable commodities that can be stored up and thereby serve as a hedge against inflation (especially gold). Gold and precious metals provide no income. They offer price appreciation, which investors realize once the asset is sold. Gold comes in various forms: jewelry, coins, bullion (bars), gold mining shares, gold futures, and gold options. Our focus is on coins and bullion. The price of coins and bullion varies with the market. Investors must check for current prices with precious metals dealers, investment brokers, or coin dealers. As with other risky investments, one should determine if there is a need in one's portfolio for gold as an inflation hedge or if it would be better to use other inflationary hedges like investment property or REIT's. Always check with a qualified investment professional before you invest in gold and precious metals.

15. Collectibles

Collectibles are real assets (antiques, figurines, paintings, sculptures, old cars, coins, stamps, etc.) that can increase or decrease in value over time. The price of collectibles is driven by supply and demand as well as by the quality of the item. TV programs like PBS's "The

Antique Road Show," HGTV's antique appraisal shows, and web sites like eBay.com and Amazon.com have helped expand the market for collectibles for the average consumer.

Investment Goals

Investing to Beat Inflation

Investors must be aware that they must invest to beat the rate of inflation. Otherwise, they are only breaking even or losing money. Let's look at how inflation impacts the rate of return on your investment in the following examples.

When the current inflation rate = 3%:
1) **Bank Savings Account Rate = 2%**
   Actual rate of return received on savings = (2%—3%) = 1%. You're losing money.

2) **Money Market Rate = 3%**
   Actual rate of return received on money market = (3%—3%) = 0%. You break even.

3) **CD Rate = 5%**
   Actual rate of return received on CD = (5%–3%) = 2%. You're making 2%.

4) **Mutual Fund Rate = 10%**
   Actual rate of return received on fund = (10%–3%) = 7%. You're making 7%.

5) **Aggressive Growth Mutual Fund Rate = 54%**
   Actual rate of return received on fund = (54%–3%) = 51% . You're making 51%.

Investors can have many goals that range from short-term to long-term, as we have explored in this book. Yet the two goals that seem to be of paramount concern to most investors are education and retirement.

Investing for Education

Parents have various options they can use to save for the future (as we will explore later in this chapter). Many parents choose tax-advantaged vehicles such as the *Uniform Gift Transfer to Minors Act* (*UGMA/UTMA*) and *education IRAs*. The *Uniform Gift Transfer to Minors Act* allows parents to open a custodial account in their child's name. The earnings are taxed at a lower rate once the child reaches age 14 years old. Before then, some of the child's earnings are taxed at the parents' rate. However, once the child turns 18–21 years of age, the parents could lose control of the money, depending on their state of residence. *Education IRAs* are tax-advantaged savings programs that can allow the parents to control the funds when the child turns 18–21 years of age, which is especially helpful if the child decides not to attend college.

Some of the steps you can take to reach your educational savings and investments goals are:

- Determine the estimated cost of 4 years of college based on your child's age. However, in this chapter we will focus on the costs of college funding for a child 0–17 years old. You can also use this analysis to determine the cost of your own education.

- With the help of your investment advisor, determine which savings or investment vehicles are most suitable for your educational goals.

- Determine, with the help of an advisor, how much you will need to set aside each month.

Determining the Most Suitable Investments

Let's look at two scenarios for individuals who need to save for college education.

The Calloways

Lester and Brenda Calloway need to save an additional $50,000 for their twin sons David and Caleb (8 years old). They have already built up some funds, but in a recent visit with their new financial advisor, they calculated their total educational savings needs.

Since the boys have 10 years before they attend college, the Calloways decide, along with their investment advisor, that they can take on some moderately high risk with their investment choice. They reason that, although the stock market has fluctuated, it has outperformed other investments over longer periods of time. They decide on an aggressive-growth mutual fund that has historically outperformed the S & P 500. The fund also diversifies their money across a wide variety of small company stocks (category #3 on the Risk Tolerance Grid; see Table 5.1). The fund has historically paid over 30% annually.

Lila Robertson

Ms. Robertson has a 15-year-old daughter who is eligible for some student loan funding but not enough to cover the total cost of her education. Ms. Robertson has accumulated some tax-deferred savings through her employer, but she already has the maximum deduction allowed coming out of her check each pay period. She needs an additional $20,000 in 3 years.

Ms. Robertson talks with several financial advisors at different companies to get advice on what she should do. Because she has only 3 years to invest and cannot afford to take on a high degree of investment risk, she selects investments in category # 2 on the Risk Tolerance Grid (Table 5.1). She decides to invest in some blue-chip stock funds that will give her growth and income. The two funds that she selects have historically had a return of 12% annually. Additionally, she will allow her daughter to work part-time to earn $5,000 per year when she turns 16 years old. She can spend half and save the other half. This will give Ms. Robertson an additional $5,000 toward college expenses; therefore, she will need to save a total of $15,000.

Estimated College Cost Based on Child's Age*

Child's Age	School Year	Public College Cost 4 Years	Public College Cost Per Year	Private College Cost 4 Years	Private College Cost Per Year
17	2001–02	$37,496	$9,374	$95,951	$23,988
16	2002–03	$39,749	$9,937	$104,886	$26,222
15	2003–04	$42,128	$10,532	$111,179	$27,795
14	2004–05	$44,655	$11,164	$117,852	$29,463
13	2005–06	$47,335	$11,834	$124,923	$31,231
12	2006–07	$50,173	$12,543	$132,417	$33,104
11	2007–08	$53,183	$13,296	$140,360	$35,090
10	2008–09	$56,373	$14,093	$148,781	$37,195
9	2009–10	$59,754	$14,939	$157,708	$39,427
8	2010–11	$63,338	$15,835	$167,172	$41,793
7	2011–12	$67,140	$16,785	$177,702	$44,426
6	2012–13	$71,170	$17,193	$187,835	$46,959
5	2013–14	$75,441	$18,860	$199,103	$49,776
4	2014–15	$79,967	$19,992	$211,048	$52,762
3	2015–16	$84,766	$21,192	$223,712	$55,928
2	2016–17	$89,853	$22,463	$237,136	$59,284
1	2017–18	$95,246	$23,812	$251,363	$62,841
New born	2018–19	$100,959	$25,240	$266,443	$66,611

* P-ojections are based on a compounded inflation rate of 6%.

Table 5.4 • Determining the Estimated Cost of College

Calculating the Monthly Amount
To calculate the monthly investment amount needed to achieve your goals, you can call an advisor. If you have a calculator or computer program that can calculate present and future value, you can do this exercise on your own. Some banks and brokerage companies offer free tools that perform these calculations on their web sites. If you have an account with them as well as access to the Internet, the calculations can easily be done.

The Calloways will need to put away $125 per month to achieve their goal of $50,000 in 10 years, investing in a mutual fund that pays 30% annually. Ms. Robertson will need $377 per month to achieve her goal of $15,000 in 3 years, investing in funds that pay 12% annually.

CAUTION: The rates on the funds are not guaranteed. Past performance may not continue into the future. The hypothetical investors in the previous examples are prepared to invest a little more when their fund returns go down. Also, they will conduct periodic reviews of their portfolios with their advisors to keep investments on track.

Be sure to check with the college, government (federal and state), community and church organizations, professional organizations (sororities, fraternities), scholarship programs, etc. to get information about scholarships, grants, work-study programs, internships, and student loans.

Investing for Retirement
Planning for retirement is the key to saving for your future. The same type of calculations that were done for education savings will be needed for retirement savings. Of course, potential investors will have to determine how much risk they are willing to assume based on their personal situation, as we discussed earlier. Let's use this section to review a few of the tax-advantaged vehicles investors can use for retirement savings.

Individual Retirement Accounts (IRAs)
IRAs are personal tax-deferred accounts that allow you to save for your future. They are offered through various financial institutions. There are two types of IRAs: the traditional IRA and the Roth IRA.

A **traditional IRA** can be deductible or non-deductible. With tax-deferred IRAs, investors pay no taxes on the investments until they make withdrawals. The earliest an investor can start withdrawing from an IRA is age 59 1/2, and the latest is age 70 1/2. One must earn at least $2,000 to be able to deduct $2,000 from taxable income for the tax year 2001. New tax laws have taken effect as of July 2001 (explained later). Based on one's adjusted gross income, the IRS will gradually decrease the amount of an IRA investment that can be deducted (subtracted from gross income) if a retirement plan is used on the job. Non-deductible IRAs are for those who have reached the maximum income limits set by the IRS for married or single persons.

A new federal tax bill that was signed into law by the George W. Bush administration took effect in July 2001. It is referred to as the **Economic Growth and Tax Relief Reconciliation Act of 2001**, and numerous changes have taken place as a result of it. To become fully aware of how it will impact you, call your tax advisor or the IRS. This book will cover how the new bill impacts retirement and education investments.

Retirement Planning

The Economic Growth and Tax Relief Reconciliation Act of 2001 contains provisions that modify qualified plans and IRA rules. For example, the maximum contribution to both traditional and Roth IRAs are incrementally increased from the current amount of $2,000 annually to $5,000 annually by the year 2008. Tax payers who are at least 50 years old are allowed an additional "catchup" contribution of $500 per year in 2002—2005 and $1,000 in 2006 and thereafter.

The maximum contribution to 401(k) plans and SEPs is increased to $11,000 in 2002 and further increased in $1,000 increments annually thereafter until it reaches $15,000 in 2006. In addition, starting in 2006, this legislation permits 401(k) plans to include a "qualified Roth contribution program" that would be handled similarly to Roth IRAs. That is, while contributions to the plan could not be deducted for taxable income, certain distributions from a "qualified Roth contribution program" will not be subject to adjusted gross income limitations that presently preclude many taxpayers from taking advantage of Roth IRAs.

Education-related Deductions and Credits

The rules regarding education IRA accounts are significantly liberalized, making the use of such accounts more attractive. The annual contribution limits are increased from $500 to $2,000 per beneficiary. The phase-out range for married taxpayers filing jointly is increased to a modified adjusted gross income of $190,000—$200,000. Starting in 2002, proceeds from these accounts can also be used for elementary and secondary education, not just post-secondary education. The higher contribution limit and more liberal distribution rules are likely to increase the popularity of these accounts.

Note: Please remember to speak with your tax advisor or the IRS regarding these new programs, which incorporate specific changes over time that will impact taxpayers differently as each year goes by.

Deductions for your IRA contributions decrease on a sliding–scale from $2,000 to $0 depending on your income. The declining deduction is based on an IRS calculation (see IRS Publication 590). You can also ask your tax advisor for clarification. Table 5.5 shows how income ranges will increase through 2007 for the sliding-scale deductions. Be aware that you can deduct the full $2,000 if you do not have a retirement plan or if you have a plan and your adjusted gross income falls below the minimum.

Tax Year	Married Filing Jointly	Married Filing Separately	Single Head of Household
2000	$52,000–$62,000	$0–$10,000	$32,000–$42,000
2001	$53,000–$63,000		$33,000–$43,000
2002	$54,000–$64,000		$34,000–$44,000
2003	$60,000–$70,000		$40,000–$50,000
2004	$65,000–$75,000		$45,000–$55,000
2005	$70,000–$80,000		$50,000–$60,000+
2006	$75,000–$85,000		
2007	$80,000–$100,000		

Table 5.5 • Income Levels for Traditional IRA Contributions

NOTE: If your spouse doesn't work, you can contribute up to $2,000 a year in a separate spousal IRA.

A **Roth IRA** is an individual retirement account that gives investors tax-free earnings on their contributions as long as the account is open for at least 5 years. This means that you owe no taxes at all on your earnings. The contributions you can make to a Roth IRA start to decline within certain ranges, depending on your tax filing status (Table 5.6). Above the maximum income levels, you cannot qualify to make a contribution to a Roth IRA, but you can still contribute to a traditional IRA account (without the deductions).

Filing Status	Married Filing Jointly	Single Head of Household	Married Filing Separately
Income Range For Sliding Scale	$95,000–$110,000	$150,000–$160,000	$0–$10,000

Table 5.6 • Income Levels for Roth IRA Contributions

To determine which IRA is best for you, speak with an investment advisor and discuss different scenarios to see which one gives you the best return based on your personal situation. As with traditional IRAs, many banks and brokerages provide software tools on their web sites that will perform these calculations for you. IRS Publication 590 also provides some insight into the detailed calculations. You can contact the IRS at 1(800) 829-1040. Remember that there are many variables to be considered when choosing an IRA.

Here are some questions you should answer when trying to decide which IRA is right for you:

1. Which IRA (Roth, tax-deductible, or non-deductible) will provide the most retirement income?
2. How will changes in my tax rate affect this decision?
3. What amount am I allowed to contribute?
4. What option is best for estate planning?
5. What if I live longer than expected?
6. What if I overestimate my return on investment?
7. When should I begin saving?
8. What effect will a large withdrawal have?
9. How will contributions to my employer's retirement plan affect my decision?
10. How will my IRA be affected if I make periodic payments through payroll deduction versus a lump-sum contribution each year?

NOTE: IRAs are investment vehicles; they are not the investment per se. Within an IRA, you can purchase various types of investments from which you will receive tax benefits because they are in the account. IRAs can contain stocks, bonds, mutual funds, CD's, and several other types of investments.

Employer Savings/Retirement Plans
There are several employer-based retirement savings plans: 401(k), 403(b), Keogh, SEP, and SIMPLE plans. The best way to find out which is best for you is to talk with your investment advisor. Let's define each type of plan to give you a general idea of how you might start the selection process or evaluate what you already have.

401(k) is a salary reduction plan that allows higher contributions than IRAs. 401(k) plans offer the possibility of receiving matching funds from your employer and reduce the income tax that you owe. However, your investment options would be limited to what is offered through the employer's plan. There is a limit to the amount of pre-tax income that can be invested in this plan. With this option, profit-sharing plans can be set up that allow employees to benefit when the company does well.

403(b) is a salary reduction plan offered to employees of non-profit organizations with optional matching contributions from employers. There is a cap on the percentage of your income that can be invested (pre-tax) with this plan.

Keogh is a plan for those who are self-employed that allows them to make tax-deductible contributions of up to 25% of their net income (up to a limit of $30,000). All earnings are tax deferred. Based on how you set up the plan with your advisor, you may have mandatory or optional contributions whether or not your company is profitable. If you have employees, you must contribute the same percentage of income as you do for yourself. Setting up a Keogh plan is complicated and will require the help of a financial professional.

SEP (Simplified Employee Plan) is a specialized IRA. For small business owners, this may be the most effective, least expensive, and least complicated way to set up a retirement plan for oneself and one's employees (if applicable). Even though SEPs are funded by the employer, they are controlled by the employee. This eliminates the cost of having an outside firm manage the plan for you. Because SEPs are qualified plans, the employer's contribution each year for himself and his employees can be deducted from the company's earnings for that year. This deduction will reduce your taxes. Contributions are optional. This is especially beneficial in lean years. The maximum contribution per employee is 15% of salary or $30,000, whichever is less. Some SEPs are salary reduction plans that allow employers and employees to contribute to the plan. All eligible employees must be included.

The **SIMPLE Plan** is an IRA plan that allows employees to contribute up to $6,000 per year. The IRS may increase this limit to keep up with inflation. Employers must contribute 2% or match up to 3% of an employee's contribution. Employees' accounts are set up as IRAs that they own. Unlike owners of other IRA accounts, who are charged a 10% IRS penalty for early withdrawal, owners of simple IRAs are charged 25% for early withdrawal. An employee's money must be in the account for at least 2 years before money can be transferred out. This program was designed in 1997 with the small business owner in mind because simple IRAs are much less complicated to administer than other forms of retirement plans.

Online Banking and Brokerage Services
This is where the financial services industry meets the web. Many investors have gone to the Internet to conduct their banking and brokerage business because of the convenience and lower cost. Many of the financial service providers who are providing investors today with regular services also provide online access to accounts for free or at a nominal cost. The following is a list of services investors can receive from online service providers.

Individuals can handle most of their **banking** needs online. For example, they can:
- Pay bills
- Transfer money between accounts
- Check balance(s)
- Make loan payments on accounts with the institution
- Find interest rates on savings products and loan programs
- Apply for new accounts
- View product information

The Urban Guide to Biblical Money Management

- Use calculators to determine the present value of investments and the future value that will be needed to achieve investment goals
- Print account statements
- Request call–backs or e–mails from bank representatives
- Set up automatic debits from their accounts
- Do research on the bank and its products

Investors can also handle most of their **brokerage** needs online. They can:
- Buy and sell stocks, bonds, and other securities
- Research investments before making investment decisions
- Study the fundamentals of investing (available on some sites)
- Calculate the present and future value of investments
- Apply for an account
- Research investment market news
- Manage portfolios
- Allocate investments among asset groups
- Receive quotes
- Review charts

With all of these services at your fingertips, you may wonder why anybody would ever call or visit their financial representative. Even with all of the innovations available on the web, many investors still need to handle service issues by telephone or in person. They may need to make deposits of physical checks or cash. Not everyone is comfortable with the Internet. Not everyone has a computer or Internet access. Most people prefer to handle large transactions (e.g., mortgage down payments, IRA or employer retirement plan roll–overs, private banking client transactions [for high net worth customers], etc.) in person. No matter what innovations are on the web, there will always be a reason to see your banker or broker in person. The Internet is a tool that can be used to make our financial lives easier. As with other tools, some will use it more than others.

The following is a list of some of the web sites dedicated to helping investors, whether large or small, evaluate the financial markets:

MUTUAL FUND WEB SITES

www.schwab.com

www.mfea.com

www.fundsinteractive.com

www.morningstar.net

www.cbs.marketwatch.com

www.quote.com

www.SmartMoney.com

www.wallstreetcity.com

STOCK MARKET WEB SITES

www.msnbc.com

www.news.com

www.nytimes.com

www.usatoday.com

www.zdnet.com

www.talks.com

www.cnnfn.com

www.abcnews.com

BOND WEB SITES

www.businessweek.com

www.investinginbonds.com

www.e–analytics.com

www.personalwealth.com

www.smartmoney.com

www.forbes.com

www.fortune.com

www.foxnews.com

www.internetnews.com/stocks

OPTIONS and FUTURES/GLOBAL WEB SITES

www.amex.com

www.altavest.com

www.nyse.com

www.lind–waldock.com

www.cboe.com

www.fadc.com

www.cbot.com

www.optionstrader.com

www.cme.com

www.marketcenter.com

www.futuresmag.com

www.ino.com

www.global-investor.com

BANKING INDUSTRY WEB SITES

www.bankrate.com

www.banxquote.com

www.ramresearch.com (offers information about credit cards)

www.mbnainternational.com (offers CD and money market rates)

www.fsn.com

www.interest.com (offers mortgage information)

"The more you know as an investor, the greater will be your ability to handle your personal and/or family finances."

IPO/DPO WEB SITES

www.ipo.com
www.directstockmarket.com
www.ipo-fund.com

www.ipomaven.com
www.witcapital.com
www.ipocentral.com

MISCELLANEOUS WEB SITES

www.dripcentral.com
www.dripinvestor.com
www.kidstock.com

ONLINE TRADING WEB SITES

www.americanexpress.com/direct
www.ameritrade.com
www.barrons.com
www.datek.com
www.dljdirect.com
www.etrade.com
www.fidelity.com
www.kiplinger.com

www.money.com
www.ndb.com
www.quick-reilly.com
www.schwab.com
www.smartmoney.com
www.wsj.com
www.waterhouse.com

When selecting an online broker:

1. If you are planning to trade only a few shares, check to see if the advertised low commission applies when less than 500 shares are purchased.

2. Check the fees charged in addition to commissions (e.g., postage and handling, transaction fees, wire service fees, stock certificate issue fees, etc.).

3. Select an online broker who handles the kind of securities you plan to trade on a regular basis; otherwise, you may end up paying more for these transactions because the broker will have to get assistance from another broker.

4. Find out about trade execution timing (the time from when you submit your buy or sell order to when the transaction is completed). Delays can be very costly.

5. Ask if excess funds from trades are automatically put (swept) into an interest-bearing account. Also ask if there are free check-writing privileges with this account.

6. Check customer service availability. Ask if there is a representative available to help you at a toll-free number and if customer service is offered by automated phone service or e-mail only. There will be times when you will need to talk to someone.

7. Ask if, in addition to customer service representatives, actual brokers will be available to assist you if the Internet site goes down or is overloaded with customers.

8. Does the broker give you "freebies" for frequent trading or for opening your account with a certain amount of money?

The difference between a full-service broker, a discount broker, and an online broker is related to fees and form of communication with the clients.

A **full-service broker** can advise individuals on various investment types and strategies for success in the market while also being able to make transactions for clients. Full-service brokers generally deal with high-net-worth clients; as a result, they are the most expensive on a cost per transaction basis. You pay a greater commission to buy and sell investments.

A **discount broker** can handle buy and sell orders for you but cannot give you advice. As a result, in most cases the commission fee is substantially less than for a full-service broker.

An **online broker** handles computerized buy and sell orders from clients via the Internet. The online broker does not speak to customers at all. As a result, the commission that clients pay is much lower than that paid to a full-service or discount broker.

Summary

As our opening Scripture pointed out, people perish without knowledge. The more you know as an investor, the greater will be your ability to handle your personal and/or family finances. We have covered a vast amount of information in this chapter. We have covered everything from savings accounts to college savings to the stock and futures markets. We have also covered how to invest on-and offline. The purpose was to inform you about some of the plethora of resources available to you. As you invest, please use this chapter as a reference guide to help you navigate through the financial markets jungle.

Questions

1. What did Hosea 4:6 say happens to people who lack knowledge?

2. Why is knowledge such an important key to investing for your future?

3. Give an example of two investment types in each of the four categories on the Risk Tolerance Grid (Table 5.1).

4. Mrs. Barnes is an unemployed 60–year–old widow who inherited $100,000 from her husband's retirement plan. What percentage of her inheritance should she put in each category of the Risk Tolerance Grid?

5. Frank and Eleanor want to save money to send their 7–year–old daughter to a private college. In what category (or categories) of the Risk Tolerance Grid should they invest their monthly payroll deductions?

6. Describe two types of investments in each of the following categories: stocks, bonds, mutual funds, and bank savings instruments.

7. What are IPO's and DPO's?

8. Name three of the riskiest investments on the market.

9. What is the difference between a traditional IRA and a Roth IRA?

10. What is the difference between an education IRA and a UGMA/UTMA custodial account?

11. Describe two types of employer retirement savings plans.

12. What is the difference between a full-service broker, a discount broker, and an online broker?

13. Name three different types of service you can receive from an online broker.

14. If the inflation rate is 3%, your mutual fund had an annual return of 20%, your high-yield bond returned 11%, and your money market account returned 5%, how much would your actual return be on each of these investments? (Show your calculations.)

Mutual fund:

High-yield bond:

Money market account:

Chapter 6

◆◆◆

HOME OWNERSHIP AND INVESTMENT PROPERTY MATTERS

In this chapter, we will focus on buying versus renting, determining how much property one can afford, calculating the costs and other items associated with purchasing real estate, using real estate professionals, and shopping for a mortgage. We will also cover purchasing investment and multi-unit property and purchasing property on the Internet.

Joshua 1:9-11

⁹ I hereby command you: Be strong and courageous; do not be frightened or dismayed, for the Lord your God is with you wherever you go. ¹⁰ Then Joshua commanded the officers of the people, ¹¹ "Pass through the camp and command the people: 'Prepare your provisions; for in three days you are to cross over the Jordan, to go in to take possession of the land that the Lord your God gives you to possess.'"

In this Scripture, land is a sign of strength, power, courage, and God's favor. Notice that the Children of Israel were told to be strong and courageous. Why was this so necessary, especially considering the fact that God had already given this land to them? It would seem that it would only then be a matter of going in, selecting their portions of the land, setting up camp, and living happily ever after. Well, there was one slight problem with this scenario: other people lived in the land. In order to get to plans B, C, and D, they first had to accomplish plan A—getting the other people off their land. Of course, this matter could have been addressed by God prior to their arrival. However, God decided to involve the Children of Israel in the process of taking possession of the land for themselves.

Isn't that just like God—involving us in our own victory, instead of just letting us sit back and watch Him do all the work? There is a reason for this: It makes us wiser and tougher so that we will have a firm foundation of past experiences to stand on. Of course, none of our past experiences could ever outdo God, yet there is something about these experiences that God uses to help us stay on track with our lives as well as our finances. In today's times, property ownership represents wisdom, some financial knowledge, prestige, and higher net worth. Like the Children of Israel, we are also faced with the challenge of taking possession of the land (property), but in a different way because in most cases other people live on or own the property we want to possess. If we have been successful in handling the smaller financial experiences of our past, we can use those experiences as stepping stones to handling the larger financial experience of real estate purchase.

Many of the keys we need to unlock the door to our dream of home ownership or investment property ownership, have been covered in earlier chapters. Planning ahead, budgeting, maintaining good credit habits, and using appropriate investments to save for future goals are some of the keys. In addition, we need to seek out the wise counsel of a good legal advisor, real estate agent, and appraisal professional. Developing the ability to do your own research regarding property value, neighborhoods, interest rates, and property taxes would also be extremely helpful, especially before taking possession of your dream property.

Purchasing property can provide many advantages. Some of these advantages are:

- **Income** Rent paid to you for leasing/renting your property or a portion of it.
- **Capital Appreciation** An increase in the value of your property (investment) recognized through its sale or exchange.
- **Tax Advantages** A shelter to ease your current and future tax liabilities with deductions for interest and property tax. The building is depreciable, and operating expenses are also deductible if the building is held as an investment.
- **Security** A roof over your head today as well as future income and profit.

Renting Versus Owning

Renting generally works in favor of the landlord in the long run. In other words, it's a win/lose situation in which somebody other than the person who is renting is winning. While not everyone can venture out on their own and buy property as soon as they become an adult, property ownership should be a primary goal. Although many things can preclude us from taking this important step in our financial lives, we must still discover ways to overcome the roadblocks. We covered some methods in earlier chapters.

Divorce, medical emergencies, past credit problems, and a limited income are at the forefront of the obstacles that hold us back. Yet even with these obstacles, we can find a way to scrape up the money to rent from somebody else. In many cases, the rent is more than, equal to, or perhaps a little bit less than what we would pay on a monthly mortgage for ourselves. However, paying **rent** doesn't give us any tax advantages, income, or future profits. Rent is paying for someone else's roof over your head, while also giving them the distinct privilege of getting wealthy with your money.

I know many people think that's easy for me to say because of all of my time working in the financial services industry, training and consulting with individuals and businesses. They think that because I've studied finances and economics in Europe and on Wall Street, I live in an ivory tower and couldn't possibly know what they are going through. Well, the situation is this: I know a woman who was divorced and welfare-ridden, non-degreed, and left with three birth children, an adopted son, a mortgage payment, and a dog to take care of. By the grace of God, she faithfully and cleverly took on extra jobs to bring in money to take care of her family, the mortgage, and her tithes: real fancy jobs like cleaning a Catholic parsonage, working the third shift at White Castle cashiering and cleaning, then moving up to take on cashiering duties at a local hospital.

She taught her children to work part-time jobs while also giving primary attention to their schooling. Because of her budgeting habits and her faithfulness to God, she not only kept the property that was left to her in her divorce, but went on years later to purchase mixed-use commercial property in great condition and in a wonderful location. She purchased the property in her own name and set up her own business on-site. In other words, she was able to collect rent in two ways: from individual tenants who rented her apartments, and from the business that leased her commercial space. By the way, every birth child attended college and is a homeowner today because of her living example of faithfulness. That woman is my mother.

No matter what your situation, there is a way out of the renting cycle if you will put your mind to it and use some of the strategies that we discussed earlier.

Action Plan
Focus on achieving the following:

- Calculate how much house you can afford (which we will do in the next section). You can also get free assistance from financial institutions that pre-qualify you.
- Research the prices of homes in various areas through real estate publications, and local newspapers and with a real estate agent.
- Select one or two properties that fit within your budget and meet your requirements.
- Research current interest rates to find out which organization(s) can offer you the best deal.
- Ask the loan officer at the mortgage company or financial institution to calculate the down payment required and the closing costs, given your current credit status.
- Review your budget and savings (individual savings, company savings, etc.) to see how much you can afford, how much you need to save, and how much you need to borrow.
- If possible, make an offer on the property for less than the asking price, of course.
- When your offer is accepted, secure a mortgage with the company that gives you the best rate. It is strongly suggested that you get the mortgage *before* negotiating for a home, because this gives you more leverage to ask the seller to reduce the asking price
- Choose a qualified real estate attorney. Get referrals from other homeowners.
- Set the closing date with your attorney.

How Much House (Property) Can You Afford? (Pre-Qualification)
Pre-qualification is the process of calculating the loan amount you can afford. Use Table 6.1 to estimate the monthly payment you can qualify for.

1. Total monthly gross income		$ _____
2. Multiply by the qualifying percentage (36%)	+	.36*
3. Amount of income available for monthly payments	=	$ _____
4. Subtract current total monthly loan payments	−	$ _____
(Credit cards, car payments, consumer loans, etc.)		
5. Total monthly payment you may qualify for	=	$ _____
6. Deduct monthly taxes and insurance**		$ _____
7. Monthly principal and interest payment after taxes and insurance	=	$ _____

*Your monthly debt payments should not exceed 36% of your monthly gross income.
**Amounts vary by location. Use 15% of line 5 as an estimate if you don't know the exact figure.

Table 6.1 • Monthly Principal and Interest Payments

How Much Can You Borrow?

Find your monthly principal and interest payment (Table 6.1, line 7) on Table 6.2 to see how much you may be able to borrow. For example: a loan of $80,000 at 7% interest with a down payment of 20%, one point (1% of the mortgage amount), and other prepaid fees of $703 would result in an APR of 7.099 and a 30-year loan with 360 payments of $533 per month.

The Urban Guide to Biblical Money Management | 105

Interest Rate	6%	6.5%	7%	7.5%	8%	8.5%	9%
APR*	6.093%	6.596%	7.099%	7.602%	8.105%	8.609%	9.112%
Mortgage Amount	\multicolumn{7}{c}{Monthly Payment}
$60,000	$360	$380	$400	$420	$441	$462	$483
$80,000	$480	$506	$533	$560	$588	$616	$644
$100,000	$600	$633	$666	$700	$734	$769	$805
$120,000	$720	$759	$799	$840	$881	$923	$966
$140,000	$840	$885	$932	$979	$1,028	$1,077	$1,127
$180,000	$1,080	$1,138	$1,198	$1,259	$1,321	$1,385	$1,449
$220,000	$1,320	$1,391	$1,464	$1,539	$1,615	$1,692	$1,771

Table 6.2 • Monthly Principal and Interest Payments

*APR Annual Percentage Rate, or the actual annual cost of credit. The APR represents the total finance charge (interest, loan fees, and points) as a percentage of the total loan amount.

Many people get this pre-qualification process mixed up with the pre-approval process. **Pre-approval** means you are actually approved for a specific loan amount. In addition, you'll receive a loan commitment letter from the mortgage company. Many people do this before they make an offer to purchase property because having a pre-approval letter will give them more leverage to negotiate for a lower purchase price.

Closing Costs

Closing costs can creep up on you if you don't estimate and save for them beforehand. These costs are in addition to the down payment and are calculated as some predetermined percentage of the total mortgage amount (e.g., 3%, 5%, 10%, or 20%). Closing costs are usually about 3%– 5% of the original mortgage amount. Both the down payment and closing costs are payable at the time of closing.

Let's look at the costs you will likely to incur when closing on a real estate transaction.

- Initial mortgage payment
- Loan origination fee (charged by lender)
- Loan discount (points charged by lender; 1 point = 1% of the mortgage amount)
- Prepaid mortgage insurance (if required)
- Attorney's fees
- Credit report fee
- Property survey
- Inspections of property fees
- Mortgage recording tax
- Prepaid homeowner's insurance for first year
- Prorated property taxes for the current year
- Closing company
- Recording deed

Don't worry about trying to keep track of all these fees on your own. Between the lender, the real estate agent, and your attorney, you will be prepared for the closing.

Example: Mortgage Amount = $100,000, Closing Costs = 5%, and Down Payment = 10%

Closing Costs + Down Payment = 5% + 10% = 15%

15% x $100,000 = $15,000 needed to close your loan.

You may want to set up a separate savings account just to achieve this goal.

Using Real Estate Professionals

When buying, use a buyer's agent. The following is a list of some of the key things a professional real estate agent should do for you:

1. Prepare a checklist of your needs and wants with respect to a new property.
2. Prequalify you for a home/property so you will know what you can afford.
3. Help you find suitable financing.
4. Schedule appointments to view homes/properties.
5. Research and provide information on the neighborhoods that interest you.
6. Research competitive offers found in published advertisements from other real estate companies.
7. Act as a liaison between you and the seller, including negotiating and presenting your offers.
8. Inform you about a warranty deed.
9. Prepare you for closing with a checklist and possible recommendations for appraisers, building inspectors, title company, insurance agents, etc.

Shopping for a Mortgage

There are a variety of mortgage financing options you can use to meet your needs. The following is a list of the types of mortgages you can use:

1. First-time Home Buyer (FHA/VA) Government Mortgages

FHA and VA mortgage programs are set up by the government to assist first-time home buyers who do not have enough cash saved for high down payments, e.g., 10%–20% of the total mortgage amount. FHA and VA loans are offered through most lenders. With **Federal Housing Authority (FHA) mortgage** loans, you can put down as little as 3% of the purchase price. With **Veterans Administration (VA)** mortgage loans, qualified veterans can avoid a down payment altogether. Income and housing price limitations usually apply and will vary depending on location. Check with your mortgage lender.

2. Conventional Mortgages (Fixed- and Adjustable-Rate)

If you plan to own your property for a number of years and prefer the certainty of fixed monthly mortgage payments, the **fixed-rate mortgage** loan program is for you. This mortgage type gives you a fixed rate over the life of your mortgage loan. The most common terms are 15 and 30 years. Also available are terms of 5, 10, 20, and 25 years.

> *"If borrowers must use sub-prime lenders, they should still do research to determine which lender will give them the most competitive rate."*

If you prefer a lower monthly payment, are not planning on owning your property for very long, or strongly believe that rates are going to go down substantially, the **adjustable-rate mortgage** program is your mortgage choice. Adjustable-rate mortgages carry lower interest rates than fixed-rate mortgages. This choice could also help you afford a more expensive property because your monthly payments will be lower due to the lower interest rates. The tradeoff is that the low rate is only fixed for a short period of time, after which the mortgage holder could be subject to rate increases or faced with refinancing. Loan terms of 1, 3, 5, 7, and 10 years are available. While the entire loan term may be 30 years, the adjustable period is the only time during which the mortgage will be fixed. After that, the mortgage rate is subject to change periodically, e.g., once every year.

3. 203(k) Mortgage/Renovation Loans

A 203(k) mortgage loan is an FHA loan that provides funds for both home financing and renovation. If you are planning to purchase a "fixer-upper," this program allows you to borrow the money you'll need all at once. After the loan closing date, renovation funds are held in a managed account. You will earn interest on these funds until it is time to pay your contractor(s). Any remaining funds can be used to make additional improvements or pay down your mortgage principal. Your loan amount will be based on the value of your home after renovation is completed. Additionally, you can take advantage of the FHA's low down payments of 3% to 5%.

4. Sub-Prime Mortgages

Sub-prime mortgage programs are designed to assist the borrower who has current credit problems or has faced such problems in the past. Because the mortgage company assumes increased risk when making these loans to credit-challenged individuals, it must charge an interest rate higher than the conventional mortgage rate. There is a greater chance of loss to the company. If borrowers must use sub-prime lenders, they should still do research to determine which lender will give them the most competitive rate. They must also review whether this loan type is affordable for them after the high rates and loan fees are added on.

Many sub-prime lenders charge extremely high fees to process loans and require much larger down payments, e.g., 10% 50% of the mortgage amount. If you absolutely *must* take this route to get mortgage financing, do your best to make this loan arrangement for as short a term as possible. Set a goal to clear up your credit and refinance at a lower rate in 1 to 3 years if possible. You can try to refinance with your mortgage lender or with a new company. Make accelerated payments on your mortgage if your budget allows.

Purchasing Investment and Multi-unit Property
Investment or multi-unit property is property you purchase purely to rent or sell later; you do not intend to stay on the premises. Investment property can be a single-family home, condominium, town house, or multi-unit property. Some individuals purchase foreclosed properties just to fix up and sell, although not all foreclosures are fixer-uppers. Multi-unit or rental properties fall into two categories: residential and commercial. **Residential rental property** contains two to four units and can be financed with a traditional mortgage loan. **Commercial rental property** contains six or more units and must be financed with a commercial loan. **Mixed-use property** combines residential and commercial space. Generally, the residential space is leased to individuals, while the commercial space is leased to businesses. This property type also requires a commercial loan, which generally calls for a larger down payment than a residential mortgage loan.

Some people opt to reside on the property while leasing out the other space(s). Be sure to do in-depth background checks on the credit and employment history of prospective tenants. This precaution will reduce the headaches and frustration that go with owning multi-unit property.

When purchasing either residential or commercial property, check the following:

Surrounding Area
- Neighborhood
- Property Values
- Community Services
- Schools
- Major Highways
- Environment
- Shopping Facilities
- Business District Types
- Transportation Resources
- City or Township Zoning Restrictions (especially if you're planning to renovate or build)

Property Exterior
- Roof
- Walls
- Trim
- Windows
- Garage
- Gutters and Downspouts
- Chimney
- Porches
- Entrances and Locks
- Landscaping

Property Interior

- Age	- Walls	- Ceiling	- Appliances
- Floor Plan	- Woodwork	- Doors	-Fixtures
- Square Footage	- Plumbing	- Ventilation	- Storage
- Furnace/Heating System	- Floors/Covering	- Electrical System	
- Air Conditioning System	- Windows	- Lighting	

"Taking a 15-year versus a 30-year mortgage could save you tens of thousands of dollars."

NOTE: For those of you who move into condos, co-ops, or town houses, be aware of the by-laws, current legal issues, current disputes, encumbrances, and any other issues that could make your ownership a very unpleasant situation. Try to speak with other tenants, neighbors, block clubs, community organizations, and local law enforcement agencies if possible. Meetings with the associations that oversee these group ownership arrangements are generally required before closing on the loan.

NOTE: Purchasing properties that are foreclosed or For Sale By Owner (FSBO) will require a greater degree of research on your part because they are not listed with a real estate agent. The usual information that is provided for you on the multiple listing sheet is not available. You will need to do research with neighbors, community organizations, law enforcement agencies, the city or township for any zoning violations on the property, the county for liens, etc. to get information, and even then the information will not be complete. Let the buyer beware (caveat emptor)! Many have purchased these properties and have lost a great deal of money. Others have reaped huge rewards. If this route is your choice, do as much research as possible before you leap in. Most of the profits in this arena are being made by very savvy real estate investors.

NOTE: Taking a 15-year versus a 30-year mortgage could save you tens of thousands of dollars. Making accelerated payments on a 30-year mortgage could also save you a substantial amount of money.

Purchasing a Home on the Internet

You can do research on the types of home and mortgage financing you want over the Internet. With the Internet, you can house hunt in your neighborhood or across the nation without ever leaving your computer. The following steps can help you conduct your search:

- Check online newspaper ads for geographical areas of interest, e.g., www.suntimes.com, www.washingtonpost.com, www.newyorktimes.com, etc.
- Check national listings for homes over the Internet, e.g., www.cyberhomes.com or www.realtor.com.
- Check with the state for realtor organization listings.
- Check national listings that show For Sale By Owner properties e.g., www.owners.com, www.4salebyowner.com, www.buyerowner.com, www.forsalebyownernetwork.com, www.privateforsale.com, etc.

- Check the real estate brokerage and agent listings, e.g., www.century21.com, www.remax.com, www.coldwellbanker.com, etc. Many of your local agents show their listings also.

Finding financing online is also possible through most banking institutions. They even allow you to apply online. There are organizations that act as liaisons between applicants and mortgage lenders, including www.lendingtree.com, www.quickenmortgage.com, www.getsmart.com, etc.

Summary

In this chapter, we have covered various issues surrounding mortgage loans and property ownership—from renting versus owning to using real estate professionals to selecting mortgage services—to help you when making one of the largest investment decisions you will ever make. We have also covered investment property purchases and shopping for property over the Internet. Hopefully, this chapter has given you the basic tools and encouragement you need to successfully purchase your first home and/or multiple properties.

Questions

1. In Joshua 1:9-11, what were the people told to do before they took possession of the land? Why was this necessary?

2. What steps are involved today in taking possession of "the land" (property)?

3. What are three major advantages of buying property versus renting?

4. What are three things you need to know when calculating how much house you can afford based on the loan amount you qualify for?

5. What is the difference between pre-approval and pre-qualification?

6. Name seven items that make up closing costs.

7. Calculate the amount needed to close on a $100,000 mortgage with 3% closing costs and a 5% down payment. (Show your calculations.)

8. What are four things that real estate agents should do for you?

9. What is the difference between government mortgages and conventional mortgages?

10. What is a 203(k) mortgage loan?

11. What kind of customers do sub-prime lenders handle?

12. Describe the two main forms of multi-unit property.

13. Name three things for each area (surrounding area, property exterior, and property interior) that you should include on your homeowner checklist.

14. Name two web sites you can use to search for a home and secure mortgage financing.

Chapter 7

◆◆◆

ENTREPRENEURSHIP MATTERS

In this chapter, we will look at entrepreneurship as a financial planning tool for increasing income and reducing taxes. We will also cover the basics of business legal structures as they relate to your financial future.

Proverbs 22:29

"Do you see those who are skillful in their work? They will serve kings; they will not serve common people."

How well we do our work is a ministry in itself because it opens doors for us to interact with people at various levels. Even more importantly, it helps us serve our families, churches, and communities better because it also opens the door for increased compensation. The more committed we are to perfecting the work we do, the more people at higher levels within and outside of our vocations will take notice and give us opportunities. Many people are so well-equipped with knowledge in their current jobs and with life experiences that they would be outstanding leaders in their own businesses, but they just haven't taken the necessary step of faith. Others have become entrepreneurs and have reaped the benefits as a result.

Entrepreneurship as a Financial Planning Tool

When considering entrepreneurship, many people get excited about the money they will make and the flexibility they will have. Another way to look at your business is as an investment. Most investments offer some return and tax advantages. You must evaluate your business just as you would any other investment. Consider it another part of your portfolio that has to perform. As with other areas of your overall financial plan (i.e., estate plan, budget, investments allocation, etc.), you must develop a business plan. If the performance of your company is off, you must evaluate the strategies outlined in your business plan and make the changes necessary to increase productivity.

Legal Forms of Business

Businesses come in three major forms: sole proprietorships, partnerships, and corporations. Each type has different income and tax consequences.

Sole Proprietorship

A sole proprietorship is owned by one person, who may also be the only employee. The owner receives all the business profits and incurs all losses. A sole proprietorship can be formed almost instantly, as long as you meet local regulations. This is also the least costly and least complicated way of starting a business. Because of its simplicity, it is probably the most popular way to set up a new business, i.e., by an individual entrepreneur. Income earned is generally tied to the maximum production of just one individual. Taxes are paid at your personal tax rate.

Advantages
- Easy to start.
- Less government regulation.
- No additional taxes are levied on business income, unlike with corporations.
- All profits go to the sole proprietor.
- The sole proprietor makes all of the decisions without having to consult others.
- No attorney required for set-up.

Disadvantages
- Unlimited legal personal liability from business-related lawsuits. The sole proprietor can be sued and have to sell his or her business and personal assets (e.g., house and auto) to acquire the money awarded to the plaintiff.
- It can be difficult for an individual business owner to raise money.
- The rate of failure is high, usually due to lack of business management expertise, financing, and a solid business plan.
- In most cases, a sole proprietor has to handle all the jobs necessary to make the business a going concern (marketing, sales, record-keeping, strategic planning, administration, etc.) without help.

Taxes
- Income tax
- Self-employment tax
- State sales tax if you are selling products (not applicable if you are providing service)

Partnerships

If you have founding members of your business or require the ongoing expertise of one or more additional professionals in your day-to-day operations, a partnership may be the route for you. Partnerships are organizations that give several individuals control of the business based on percentages set forth in a legal document known as a partnership agreement. The percentages of ownership are usually determined before the formation of this

> *"It is usually a good idea not to assign equal percentages to partners"*

business entity. Partners are valuable because they can offer various resources, (e.g., experience, money, an active client or customer list, etc.).

It is usually a good idea not to assign equal percentages to partners so that the business doesn't wind up gridlocked when voting on how to move forward on projects. Be sure to be diligent in researching an individual's business habits and personality before you make him or her a partner in your business. If a partner does not give you the desired outcome, you cannot fire him or her. You will have to go through time-consuming and costly legal procedures to get rid of the person. Many liken bad partnerships to bad marriages. Many have also dubbed partnerships as the worst form of business, compared with sole proprietorships and corporations.

Advantages
- Additional capital (money) can be invested in the business by a partner.
- Better decision-making ability with more expertise.
- Can spread out workload to gain more efficiency in operations.
- Can increase company's income through access to a larger client or customer base.
- Legal fees are lower than those needed to create a corporation.

Disadvantages
- Legal fees for creating a partnership are higher than those incurred for a sole proprietorship.
- It can be difficult to get rid of a bad partner.
- The very survival of the entire business is tied to the decisions of each general partner, even if the decisions are bad.
- Bankruptcy or other financial hardships of one partner can endanger the survival of the business.

Taxes
- Income tax (split based on personal income earned)
- Self-employment tax
- State sales tax if you are selling products (not applicable if you are providing a service)

Corporation
Of the three legal forms of business, a corporation is the most complicated and costly form of business to start. It has shareholders who own stock in the company. Separate from its shareholders, it has a management team that is responsible for the day-to-day operations of the organization. It also has a board of directors who are responsible for overseeing the management team as well as hiring and firing management team members. The company must follow certain rules to be in compliance with federal, state, and local regulations. Also, taxes have to be filed each year during specific periods designated by the IRS.

You can be the chairman of the board, the president, or one of several other officers in your corporation so that you maintain control. However, it is strongly advisable that you hire experienced professionals to oversee duties that you do not have the expertise to carry out. Even if you do have expertise in several areas, you may still want to hire others to take on these responsibilities and thereby ease the load on yourself so that you can lead your company. Some people choose the subchapter S corporation to combine the features of limited liability to shareholders and transfer of income and losses that flow to you, as in a sole proprietorship or partnership. Check with your attorney or accountant to see if this or another form of business is best for you.

Advantages
- The shareholder(s) has limited liability. Only the corporation can be sued for its assets, not the individual owners.
- You can raise funds to operate your company by distributing shares to shareholders.
- You can maintain control of your company.
- You have the ability to hire and fire when necessary.
- Loans are made to the company, which protects you from personal liability if the company goes out of business or bankrupt.
- You have increased income potential with more professionals working for you.

Disadvantages
- This is the most costly form of business.
- This is the most complicated form of business to run.
- Ongoing accounting, legal, and tax-reporting obligations are considerably more demanding (time-consuming and expensive).
- It can be very challenging to pay competitive salaries to competent professionals.
- Putting together an experienced board of directors is also a challenge.
- If you are a new business with no track record, it can be very difficult to find a financial institution willing to give you a business loan. You may end up having to use a personal loan to finance your business, which exposes you to legal liability if your business doesn't make it.
- Distribution of dividends to shareholders results in double taxation. The company pays taxes on income, then this same income is taxed again as dividends paid to the shareholder. Most small companies don't have this issue.

Taxes
- Personal income tax
- Corporate tax
- Tax on dividends

Whatever form of business you decide on, make sure you check with a qualified accountant and attorney to evaluate what is best for you in light of your personal situation. Remember that we are looking at businesses as an asset designed to produce income and tax advantages in addition to all other benefits.

Tax Benefits Available to All Legal Forms of Home-Based Businesses
Whether your decision is to form a sole proprietorship, partnership, or corporation, when operating this business from your home you can reap great advantages that will reduce your taxable income. You can receive deductions for a percentage of your utilities used, maintenance fees, mortgage payments or rent, assessments, etc. These deductible amounts will be based on the percentage of your home used to conduct business. This location must be designated exclusively for your business. You can also receive tax deductions for the use of your car, office equipment purchased (through depreciation), supplies, training, subscriptions, and fees to professional organizations. Of course, there is a deduction for business travel and entertainment, which includes lodging, meals, and transportation.

NOTE: The IRS allows you to claim deductions for depreciation of real estate, autos, and office equipment that you own. For example: If you purchase a new car, you can depreciate this asset in equal amounts (straight-line depreciation) over a specific time period or in amounts that are greater in the first years and decline over time (accelerated depreciation). Let's say that the cost of a new car that you use for business is $30,000. You can depreciate this asset in one of two ways (Table 8.1).

Auto Cost	Straight-Line Depreciation (5 Years) Annual Deduction	Accelerated Depreciation (3 Years) Annual Deduction
$30,000	$6,000 / Year	$15,000 in year 1, $10,000 in year 2, $5,000 in year 3

Table 8.1 • Example of Asset Depreciation

Check with your tax advisor to get the depreciation schedule that is appropriate for you, because these schedules vary depending on the asset you are depreciating.

Summary

We have covered the various legal forms of business, along with their advantages and disadvantages. We also looked at the tax treatment of each of these forms of business and how each business type can impact your income. In addition, we covered specific tax advantages available to home-based businesses as well as an example of depreciation and its impact on your tax deductions.

Questions

1. What point is made in Proverbs 22:29 about faithfulness in your work or business?

2. Describe the three legal forms of business.

3. Name three advantages and disadvantages of each form of business.

4. Name two types of taxes associated with each form of business.

5. Name seven types of tax deductions available to home-based businesses.

6. How does depreciation work for you?

7. If you run a home-based business and just purchased a car for $40,000 that will be used for your business, how much can you deduct for depreciation if you use a 5-year depreciation schedule? (Use the space below to calculate.)

Section IV

♦

SHELTERING YOUR FUTURE

(1 Timothy 5:8)

"And whoever does not provide for relatives, and especially for family members, has denied the faith and is worse than an unbeliever."

God is very serious about our responsibility to take care of our families, especially those in our immediate household. Our family's future is nothing to toy around with. Preparing for and sheltering your future takes much planning and discipline to stay on track with your goals. The greater portion of 1 Timothy 5 focuses on caring for the needs of others as an integral part of our Christian duty. This honors God, lest we be categorized with someone who has no belief in God at all.

In this final section, we will review "Insurance, Wills, and Estate Planning" and "Tax Matters" in Chapters 8 and 9, respectively. We will outline the process for determining life insurance needs as well as for comparing life insurance programs. We will also cover how wills and estate plans can help you and your family. Finally, we will look at strategies to help avoid and reduce taxes.

Chapter 8

◆◆◆

INSURANCE, WILLS, AND ESTATE PLANNING

The issues we will cover in this chapter are key to preparing your family (as independents) for the future. We will cover the basics of evaluating one's life insurance needs and the types of life insurance available. We will also cover the importance of establishing a will and an estate plan and what these instruments are designed to do.

Proverbs 13:22
"The good leave an inheritance to their children's children, but the sinner's wealth is laid up for the righteous."

God gave us our families, and it is important to Him that we take care of them today and in the future. Psalm 127:3 states that "... children are an heritage of the Lord and the fruit of the womb is his reward" (KJV). It is imperative that we make provisions for our child(ren), spouse, and others who depend on our wages. There are many cases in which financially ill-equipped spouses and dependent children have gone into poverty because no plan was put together to handle their needs. Sometimes, an elderly person has to return to work to make ends meet when his or her spouse dies or suffers a major physical disability. Insurance, wills, and estate planning are an important part of financial planning.

Evaluating How Much Life Insurance You Need

For those who support a family, keep a household running, have a mortgage, and/or expect children to go to college, insurance can fill the gap left by death or disability. If you do not have dependents, your life insurance needs will be different. Generally, people need less insurance as they enter their senior years because financial obligations have been settled. With surviving dependents, having enough insurance to cover living expenses and cash needs is imperative for their stability. The amount of insurance needed will vary based on the number of dependents, lifestyle, and other sources of income.

Table 7.1 shows how to calculate how much insurance one needs.

1. Dependents' annual living cost mortgage and other loan payments	+	$ _____

2. Dependents' sources of income
    -Salary
    -Investment Income
    -Social Security/Pension, etc.
	−	$ _____

3. Additional income needed (Subtract line 2 from line 1)	=	$ _____
4. Divide line 3 by the prevailing interest rate (the average rate you can get on your investments)	÷	.06
5. The amount of insurance you need	=	$ _____

Coverage can be increased to provide money for other expenses.

Table 7.1 • Calculating Insurance Needs

Now let's look at a real-life example in Table 7.2.

1. Dependents' annual living cost
   mortgage and other loan payments*   + $ 57,000

2. Dependents' sources of income**
   -Salary   ($25,000)
   -Investment Income   ($2,000)
   -Social Security / Pension, etc. ($0)   − $ 27,000

3. Additional income needed
   (Subtract line 2 from line 1)   = $ 30,000

4. Select a current average market rate available
   (the average rate you can get on your investments)   ÷   .06

5. The amount of insurance you need
   Divide line 3 by the prevailing interest rate***   = $500,000

*Use these expense numbers from your monthly budget and multiply them by 12 months to get the annual amount needed for line 1.

Table 7.2 • Sample Insurance Calculations

**Add the annual salary, investment income, pension income, and any other income together to get the total income amount needed for line 2.

***$30,000 / .06 = $500,000.

124 | The Urban Guide to Biblical Money Management

Insurance Types

Term Insurance (Renewable versus Level)

Term insurance is the least expensive way to provide life insurance for oneself. It can be purchased annually or for a specific period of time such as 10 or 15 years. If you are alive when the coverage expires, there is no payout to beneficiaries. If you die before the coverage expires, beneficiaries will be able to collect on the policy. With decreasing term policies, the face value of the policy declines over the years, giving you less coverage at the end of the policy when you least need it. When you compare the rates for term insurance, check the cost per $1,000 of death benefits. Some companies give you a discount when you purchase larger amounts of insurance for longer terms.

Renewable term life insurance policies can be renewed annually, with premiums that increase each year.

With **level term** life insurance policies, premium payments are fixed for the entire term of the policy, e.g., 10 or 15 years. Although the premiums start out higher than those for renewable term policies, level policies are less expensive in the long run. For example: If a 40-year-old woman needed $300,000 of coverage for the next 15 years, how would the different term policy programs impact her premium payments? If the insurance company charges $515 in the first year with payments increasing to $1,000 in year 15 for a renewable policy and $600 per year for a level policy, less money would be paid out with the level policy.

Cash Value Insurance (Whole Life, Universal Life, and Variable Life)

Cash value policies are different from term policies in that they carry a death benefit plus tax-deferred savings. Part of your premium builds up a tax-deferred cash reserve. If you surrender the policy, you get the cash reserves back. Your beneficiaries get the death benefit when you die. If you surrender the policy, you can keep part of the cash reserve. This is known as the surrender value. If the cash reserve is taken before age 59 1/2, you will owe taxes. If the policy is held until death, your beneficiaries will owe no income tax on payments received.

There are three primary kinds of cash value insurance: whole life, universal life, and variable life.

Whole life insurance is the traditional insurance policy we are used to hearing about. It is sometimes called straight life insurance. Premiums remain constant for the full length of the policy. When all premiums have been paid, your policy remains effective until you die. A cash reserve is accumulated, but you have no input as to how it will be invested; only the insurance company handles that matter.

Universal life insurance gives you much more flexibility than whole life insurance. You can vary the amount of the premium that goes into savings as well as increase or decrease the amount of the death benefit while the policy is active. This flexibility will cost you more in

> *"be careful if you are using or considering using insurance as an investment vehicle."*

higher premiums to cover administrative costs. Generally, the first year of a universal life policy offers a fixed rate of return on the investment portion, while the rate will vary during the remaining years of the policy. This rate will have a minimum level.

Variable life insurance is set up for investing. You choose where to invest your cash value from options made available through the insurer. Your policy value is based on how well your investments do.

Evaluate your insurance needs on a periodic basis because they usually decline over time. People end up paying unnecessary premiums when they don't reevaluate. Also, be careful if you are using or considering using insurance as an investment vehicle. Insurance was originally designed for protection, not investment. Investing through insurance policies is much more costly than investing on your own due to high administrative and commission fees charged by the insurance company. For this reason, many people have canceled their policies in exchange for a more traditional, less expensive policy while investing on their own with an investment advisor and rather than an insurance agent.

Generally, **group life insurance** offered through the employer is the least expensive insurance program for individuals and family members. Many working people use this as their life insurance option.

Long-Term Care Insurance

It is very important to set up some type of insurance in case disability and/or a catastrophic illness occurs. Your family will still need income if they depended on you before an illness or long-term disability. In this case, **disability insurance** is key because it will provide a percentage of your income for you and your family. **Catastrophic insurance** covers additional medical costs after your regular health insurance has ended. Of course, anyone who qualifies for Social Security also qualifies for **Medicare** at age 65.

Wills

A **will** is a legal document that transfers what you own to your beneficiaries when you die. It also designates the funds or assets that should be used to pay your estate or inheritance taxes. The will names the **executor**, who will handle carrying out the terms of your will. It also names a **guardian** who will care for your minor children, if applicable. A **trustee** is the person or institution that manages any trusts you have established and/or the assets left to your children, if applicable. A will should be made as soon as you purchase or inherit real estate, get married, and especially when you have children. If you do not have a will when you die, you are intestate. The state will determine what happens to your estate and your minor children through the probate court, which is an extremely slow and costly process. Living wills express your wishes about being kept alive if terminally ill or seriously injured.

Changes to Your Will
There will be times when you will need to update your will to reflect your current situation, e.g., the birth of a child, marriage, divorce, increased personal wealth, or just a change of mind. Minor changes to a will are done with a **codicil** (a written amendment that you sign and date before witnesses). Major changes require a new will, which supersedes the old will. Destroy your old will and its copies to avoid confusion and longer settlement periods. If you decide to leave people out of your will, you can legally do so (with the exception of your spouse) unless you reside in a state with laws that govern community property. To disinherit your children, you must state this in your will. Other persons can simply be omitted, or you can leave them $1 to express your feelings for them.

A well-drawn-up will can save your heirs thousands of dollars in estate taxes and can ensure that the things you have worked so hard for won't end up with someone else.

In addition to the benefits listed earlier, a will allows you to:

- Take advantage of financial planning techniques that will minimize overall estate taxes for you and your spouse.
- Ensure the proper handling of particular assets, such as a closely held business, collectibles, or family heirlooms.
- Indicate at what age you want your children to receive their inheritance.

To avoid high costs when drafting a will, prepare your information before you see an attorney. You can actually draw up a document stating your choices for guardian, executor, trustee, etc. that includes all other pertinent information you desire to present to an attorney. This will reduce the time and money you have to spend on this process.

Estate Planning

Estate planning allows you to design a comprehensive plan using gifts, trusts, and other strategies to disburse your assets. Proper estate planning will help to avoid tremendously large tax bills. The more assets you own, the more important it is to have an estate plan.

How To Save Your Heirs' Money
After spending all of your life building up your assets, it may seem strange that you will have to deplete them as much as possible to save your heirs taxes.

Bypass Trusts
With this vehicle you can pass up to $600,000 tax free on to your heirs after your surviving spouse's death. This trust exists independently and is not considered a part of your spouse's estate. For example: If your estate was worth $850,000, your spouse could receive $250,000 tax free due to the unlimited marital deduction. The rest of the assets could be put into a trust for children or grandchildren.

Tax-Free Gifts

You and your spouse could each designate up to $10,000 in cash or property as tax-free gifts to anyone you want. For example: Each parent could give $10,000 per year to a child, for a total of $20,000 annually. If the parents had two children, the total they could give would be $40,000. If they did this for 10 years, the total would equal $400,000. This could reduce an $850,000 estate to $450,000 of taxable assets.

Life Insurance

If you set up your insurance policy so that you are not the owner, you can avoid estate taxes because the death benefit won't be added to your estate. Policy ownership can be assigned to someone else. Have someone else buy the policy on your life—make sure they like you—and you can pay the premiums. You can also set up a trust to own the policy.

What does your estate contain?
- Everything in your name, e.g., bank accounts, real estate, life insurance, and investments.
- Half of everything you own jointly with your husband or wife.
- All that you own jointly with another person unless there is proof that the other person paid.
- Your share of any partnership or other business.
- Property in custodial accounts or revocable trusts that you created and for which you are the custodian or trustee.
- Money owed to you.

What liabilities reduce your estate?
- Your outstanding debts.
- Taxes you owe.
- The costs of settling the estate.

The total value of your estate is calculated to determine how much your heirs owe in federal estate taxes and state inheritance taxes. The tax consequences will vary depending on how you give your assets away. You can give your assets as a gift while you are still alive or as an inheritance after you are deceased. Get a competent estate planner to calculate which method of distribution is best for you.

Questions

1. What does Proverbs 13:22 say that the righteous do for their children's children?

2. What is the purpose of evaluating how much life insurance you need?

_____
_____
_____
_____
_____
_____

3. Describe the two main types of term insurance.

_____
_____
_____
_____

4. What are the three main types of cash value insurance?

_____
_____
_____
_____
_____
_____

5. If your dependents' annual living expenses are $50,000 and their sources of income total $15,000, calculate the additional amount of income you would need as well as the face value of an insurance policy you would need. The current interest rate is 8%.

1. Dependents' Annual Living Expenses			$ _____
2. Dependents' Sources of Income	–		$ _____
3. Additional Income Needed	=		$ _____
4. Current Interest Rate	x		.08
5. Face Value of Policy Needed	=		$ _____

Use this space for your calculations.

6. What is the difference between a cash value policy and a term life policy?

7. What can you do with a variable life policy that you cannot do with a whole life policy?

8. Name three things that a will does for you.

9. In a will, what terms are used to indicate who handles your children and who manages the assets in your estate?

10. What does an estate plan do for you?

11. Name three things that an estate contains.

12. Describe one of the types of estate plans covered.

Chapter 9

◆◆◆

TAX MATTERS

This chapter will cover some of the creative planning strategies one can use to lower taxes. The chapter will also cover key issues in selecting record-keeping methods and tax professionals that meet your needs and your budget. It will also cover some questions you should ask before choosing a tax advisor.

Matthew 17:24, 27, NIV
[24] After Jesus and his disciples arrived in Capernaum, the collector of the two-drachma tax came to Peter and asked, "Doesn't your teacher pay the temple tax?" [27] (Jesus said . . .) "But so that we may not offend them, go to the lake and throw out your line. Take the first fish you catch; open its mouth and you will find a four-drachma coin. Take it and give it to them for my tax and yours."

One of the points that Jesus is making in this Scripture is that as law-abiding citizens we must follow the laws of the land. Jesus, the King of kings, who owns the cattle on a thousand hills, acknowledged that even He must pay taxes. Since Jesus didn't have a regular job with a payroll check, He came up with a creative ecclesiastical strategy to pay His taxes. While we are required as Christians to follow in Christ's footsteps and pay our taxes, there is nothing wrong with using creative strategies to pay off or avoid taxes altogether. As long as our strategies fall within the appropriate legal framework, there is no problem.

Creative Planning Strategies One Can Use to Reduce Taxes
There are a multitude of strategies one can use to reduce taxes. We will focus on a few that may be helpful to you.

Charitable Contributions

Obviously, when you pay **tithes** and **offerings** to a not-for-profit religious institution with a (501c3) designation from its state, you can receive a tax deduction if you have reached a certain giving threshold set by the IRS. You may also receive a deduction when you make **monetary contributions** to other types of not-for-profit (501c3) organizations (e.g., Boys and Girls Clubs of America, United Way, Easter Seals, Girls Scouts, etc.). While many taxpayers are aware of this information, they miss out on hundreds and even thousands of dollars of tax deductions for **non-monetary** contributions of items include clothing, furniture, appliances, office equipment, etc. The same rule establishing a minimum contribution to qualify for a tax deduction also applies when making non-monetary donations. Taxpayers must meet a minimum donation threshold set by the IRS. Check IRS Publication 526 and/or ask your tax advisor for updated information.

Charitable Activity

If you are actively involved with a qualified non-profit organization, you can deduct expenses directly related to your involvement in the organization as long as you are not reimbursed. For example: If you sing in the choir at your church, you can deduct mileage or gas expenses for traveling to church to sing or rehearse.

You can also deduct expenses for the purchase of choir robes and other uniforms used by your choir. The cost of dry-cleaning is also deductible. If you pay to travel out of town or across town to sing with the choir, your travel, lodging, and meals are deductible. The same is true for any qualified non-profit organization you volunteer for. The IRS recommends that you keep a log of every expense incurred, along with receipts. For non-monetary donations, it is up to you to reasonably estimate how much the items donated are worth. Prepare a letter for the organization you're donating to that shows the total dollar amount and items donated, get an authorized signature, and keep a copy for yourself. See IRS Publication 526.

Small Business Activity

Expenses associated with starting a small business in your home are deductible. These might include a percentage of the cost of electricity, gas, mortgage, rent, maintenance (assessments if living in a condo or co-op), etc. One can also receive deductions for equipment and supplies purchased. Of course, any travel, entertainment, and lodging that is directly associated with your business is deductible. Workshops, classes, and training materials related to your business development are also deductible. For example, if you attend a workshop conducted at a resort in Hawaii, your expenses are deductible as long as the workshop is directly related to your business activity. Even memberships in professional organizations and subscriptions to publications related to your business are deductible. Expenses incurred in paying wages to yourself and any employees are also deductible. Auto expenses and purchases are deductible to a certain extent. See IRS Publication 334.

Real Estate (Depreciation)

Depreciation gives taxpayers the opportunity to deduct a specific portion of the initial

Property Type	Purchase Price	Deduction Divider	$$ Deductible/Year
Residential	$200,000	27.5 Years	$7,273
Commercial	$500,000	39 Years	$12,821

Table 9.1 • Calculating Deductions for Depreciation

purchase price of their real estate from their adjusted gross income every year. For residential properties, one must divide the purchase price by 27.5 years to get the amount that can be deducted each year. For commercial property, one must divide the purchase price by 39 years to get the amount that can be deducted (Table 9.1).

See IRS Publications 946 and 527 (for rental properties).

Real Estate Expenses
Property taxes and interest charges qualify as deductions on federal income tax returns. If the property is held as an investment, the operating expenses are also deductible.

Equity Lines of Credit/Home Equity Loans
Equity loans and lines of credit also come with certain tax advantages. Interest on all other consumer credit (e.g., credit cards, auto loans, installment loans, etc.) is non-deductible. With equity loans and lines of credit, taxpayers can deduct up to $100,000 in interest payments based on certain specifications determined by the IRS. For this reason, many consumers pay for autos, education, vacations, home improvements, etc. with dollars borrowed through their equity loans or lines of credit. See IRS Publication 936.

Security Sales
One can avoid paying taxes on some or all of the capital gains received by selling securities that have decreased in value. The losses can be used to offset your gains and, in some cases, to offset income. If you feel that the security (stock, bond, mutual fund, etc.) is not worth holding onto, selling it not only cleans out your portfolio, it can also help turn around a losing investment strategy. See IRS Publication 544.

Shifting Income to Children
Children over age 14 have tax rates determined by their individual income. In most cases, their tax rate is lower than that of their parents. Taxpayers can shift money and investments to their children to save taxes on earnings or on the sale of property that has increased in value. Children who are under age 14 pay taxes at their own rate up to $1,100 of unearned income and at the parents' rate thereafter. See IRS Publication 929.

Record Keeping
Keeping a record of income and expenses is key to receiving appropriate tax deductions. It is very important for you to keep track of income other than your payroll check; that record keeping is provided for you by your employer. Examples of other income include: rent, business fees, investment income, and royalties earned on intellectual property (published books, copyrighted music, sound recordings, etc.) You should also keep track of your expenses so that you can itemize deductions and/or take advantage of exclusions or credits. Include explanations with your tax return if a deduction seems extraordinary to you. Keep all canceled checks and receipts.

"Keeping a record of income and expenses is key to receiving appropriate tax deductions."

Taxpayers often ask how long they should keep their records. The IRS has 3 years in which to audit your return. If income is under-reported, the IRS has 6 years. If a return is filed falsely or not at all, the IRS has forever. For this reason, it is important for you to keep certain records for an adequate period of time. Take a look at Table 9.2 to determine how long you should keep records.

Record Type	How Long You Should Keep the Records
Income and Expenses	3–7 years (7 years is best)
Intangible Investments (Non-Real Estate)	3 years
Real Estate	7 years after the property is sold
Tax Returns	7 years or more

For additional information, see IRS Publication 17.

Table 9.2 • Retaining Your Records

Selecting Tax Professionals
Most taxpayers use some type of professional service, software, or knowledgeable family members and friends to assist in preparing their taxes. Whoever you decide to use, make sure they are qualified to handle the job. Some tax preparers are certified by the U.S. Treasury Department through continuing education requirements or are accredited by the IRS, while others are accountants, Certified Public Accountants (CPA's), or Certified Financial Planners (CFP's). Take a look at Table 9.3 to compare the various types of tax preparers and the associated costs.

Agents	They charge fees of $100–$300 and are certified by the Treasury Department and accredited by the IRS. They can also represent you in an audit or appeal to the IRS. They must take continuing education courses.
Tax Preparation Services	They charge moderate fees and generally handle middle-income individuals. They prepare uncomplicated tax returns. They cannot represent you during an audit.
CPA's	They can charge $500–$2,500 or more depending on the client's situation. They usually handle professional executives and/or persons with challenging investment portfolios and financial situations. They provide in-depth tax planning throughout the year for their clients and are able to represent their clients during IRS proceedings. Not all CPA's are tax specialists.
Tax Attorneys	Clients will pay $150–$500 per hour, with total fees easily in the thousands of dollars. They advise rather than prepare taxes. They have a working knowledge of tax laws and rulings. They can represent you in IRS proceedings and in court.

Table 9.3 • **Costs of Tax Preparation**

Questions you should ask before choosing a tax advisor:

- How much will it cost if you prepare my return?
- What kind of training do you have as a tax preparer? How frequently do you receive additional training?
- Are you available all year or only during tax season?
- Is tax return preparation a regular part of your business?
- Do you have experience with tax situations similar to mine?
- How much assistance can you provide if I am audited?

NOTE: Be aware that you can follow up with the IRS to get answers to questions on your own without paying fees. However, the IRS representatives cannot advise you. You can contact the IRS at **1(800) TAX-1040** (829-1040), or at their web sites: **www.irs.gov** or **www.irs.ustreas.gov**.

Summary

In this chapter, we have covered tax planning strategies you can use to avoid or reduce taxes. Additionally, we have discussed record keeping, selecting a tax advisor to meet your needs, and questions to ask before selecting an advisor. While taxes and IRS issues are mammoth subjects to tackle, the goal of this chapter is to give you some important fundamentals to help you move forward in your tax planning.

Questions

1. What point did Jesus make about taxes in Matthew 17:24, 27?

2. Why should you use creative tax strategies?

3. What two primary types of charitable contributions can you make to receive tax deductions from the IRS?

4. Give four examples of contributions you can make to your church to receive a deduction.

5. Give three strategies (besides charitable contributions) that you can use to receive tax deductions.

6. If you take a trip to the Virgin Islands to attend a conference that is directly related to your consulting practice, what deduction category will your expenses fall under? Name three types of deductions you can claim from this trip.

7. When keeping records, what are some sources of income you should keep track of in addition to your payroll check?

8. How long should you keep your tax returns?

9. Describe two types of tax preparers.

10. List four of the seven things you should know before selecting a tax advisor.

GLOSSARY

Adjusted Gross Income — Term used by the Internal Revenue Service (IRS) to describe income after certain deductions are subtracted from gross or total income.

American Stock Exchange — The second major stock exchange in the U. S. (after the New York Stock Exchange).

Amortization — A method of paying off a mortgage.

Annual Percentage — The actual interest rate after additional fees Rate (APR) and/or compounding has been taken into account.

Asked Price — The price at which brokers are willing to sell a security to customers.

Assets — All forms of property owned by a person or business. Examples are cash, securities, real estate, collectibles, business equipment, and other things of value.

Balance Sheet — The financial statement that shows all of the assets and liabilities of a corporation or individual.

Bankruptcy — The condition in which a person is legally declared unable to pay off his or her debts.

Bear Market — Technical term for a long-running downward-moving securities market.

Beneficiary — The person who receives certain benefits as spelled out in a trust or life insurance contract.

Benefits	A payment made to a person under an insurance policy, pension plan, or annuity.
Bid Price	The price at which brokers are willing to buy securities from customers.
Blue-Chip Stock	The common stock of large, well-known, financially strong corporations with good records of earnings and dividend payments over many years.
Broker	A person in the business of buying and selling securities (or insurance policies) for another party, for which he or she receives a commission.
Budget	A financial statement that includes income and expenses.
Bull Market	Technical term for a long-running upward-moving securities market.
Capital Gains	The market increase (appreciation) in the value of securities or other assets.
Capital Loss	The market decrease in the value of securities or other assets.
Cash Surrender Value	The amount of cash available in an insurance policy for withdrawal by the owner upon termination of the policy, before death or maturity occurs.
Certified Financial Planner (CFP)	A designation given to financial planners who pass a national examination administered by the Certified Financial Planning Board in conjunction with the College for Financial Planning.
Certified Public Accountant (CPA)	An accountant who passes a national licensing examination and who is licensed in his or her own state.
Closing Costs	Costs incurred when closing a real estate transaction between two parties. Included in these costs are title insurance, attorney's fees, recording fees, and more.

Commission	The fee paid to a broker or other agent to buy or sell securities.
Compound Interest	The interest that accrues when earnings for a specified period are added to the principal, so that interest for the following period is calculated based on the principal plus computed interest.
Default	Failure to pay principal or interest when due.
Depreciation	The decline in dollar value of an asset over time through usage.
Disposable Income	Income left over after all of the expenses are paid each month.
Diversification	The strategy of reducing risk by spreading money among several different types of investments.
Dividend	Payment made to owners of common or preferred stock.
Dollar Cost Averaging	Adding fixed dollar amounts on a regular basis to one's investment over a long period of time to reduce one's average cost.
Dow Jones Industrial Average	A statistical series that shows the general level and movement of the prices of 30 securities.
Earnings Per Share	The earnings of a company over a given period of time.
Equal Credit Opportunity Act	Federal consumer credit law that prohibits discrimination against an applicant for credit because of age, sex, marital status, race, color, religion, national origin, or receipt of public assistance.
Equity	The part of an asset that one owns; for example, for a $100,000 house with a $60,000 mortgage, $40,000 is the amount of equity or ownership.

Fair Credit Reporting Act	Federal consumer credit law that sets up a procedure for the prompt correction of mistakes on the consumer's credit report and requires that the report be kept confidential.
Federal Deposit Insurance Corporation (FDIC)	A federal government agency that insures non-brokerage bank accounts placed in Federal Reserve member banks and certain other qualifying financial institutions. The insurance amount equals a maximum of $100,000 per account owner.
Gross Income	For federal income tax purposes, all income derived from whatever source, including compensation for services, rent, interest, dividends, alimony, etc.
Hedge	To protect oneself against potential investment loss by making a counterbalancing transaction.
Inflation	An economic condition in which the purchasing power of the dollar decreases. This also causes a rise in the general price level of all goods.
Interest	The compensation paid by the borrower for the use of money; generally expressed as an annual percentage rate.
Investment	The purchase of an asset with the expectation that a profit or income will be realized.
Itemized Deductions	Deductions that are used to offset income if they collectively exceed the standard deduction. These include state and local taxes, charitable contributions, etc.
Leverage	The strategy of using borrowed money in an attempt to get a higher rate of return. This strategy succeeds when the interest rate on the loan is lower than the rate of return on the investment.
Liquidity	The ease with which an investment can be quickly converted into cash.

Market Value	The dollar value that one could get for property if one were to sell it.
Maturity	The date when the principal amount of a security becomes due and is to be paid off.
Moody's	A bond rating service that assigns credit ratings to bonds to help investors assess the risk associated with buying them.
National Association of Securities Dealers (NASD)	A self-regulatory body of broker/dealer firms organized to develop, promote, and enforce standard procedures and ethical practices in the securities industry.
Net Asset Value	As applied to mutual funds, the market value of underlying securities divided by the number of outstanding mutual fund shares.
New York Stock Exchange	The largest organized stock exchange in the U.S., accounting for 78% of the total dollar volume of securities transactions on all stock exchanges.
Portfolio	The investments held by an individual or organization.
Principal	The total amount originally invested or borrowed.
Private Mortgage Insurance (PMI)	Insurance issued by a private insurance company, and used to protect the lender against the borrower's default.
Prospectus	The official statement that describes the shares of a security or mutual fund being issued.
Risk	The probability of future loss.
Securities and Exchange Commission	The federal agency with the responsibility of regulating the securities markets and all publicly held investment companies.
Security	An evidence of debt or property, such as a bond or stock certificate.

Speculate	To make an investment in spite of potentially high risks in the hope of achieving a substantial return.
Standard & Poor's (S & P)	A bond rating service that assigns credit ratings to bonds to help investors assess the risk associated with buying them. It also evaluates stocks.
Taxable Income (Net Income)	Income that is subject to federal personal income tax. Itemized deductions and personal exemptions are subtracted from adjusted gross income to calculate taxable income.
Tax-deferred Investment	An investment on which the payment of income tax is postponed. Some examples are IRA's, annuities, and U.S. savings bonds.
Tax-exempt Investments	An investment in which income is not subject to federal and/or state income tax.
Tax Shelter	Any device or investment that provides a legal means of reducing, deferring, or avoiding taxation.
Vesting	The process whereby an employee receives increasingly greater rights (usually as the length of employment increases) to retirement benefits based on contributions made to a retirement fund by the employer.
Yield	The measurement of the profitability of invested resources; the net annual percentage of income from an investment or return. Also known as return on investment. Yield The measurement of the profitability of invested resources; the net annual percentage of income from an investment or return. Also known as return on investment.

APPENDIX

Table 2.1 • A Simple Goal Matrix

Today's Date:

GOAL	AMOUNT NEEDED		DATE NEEDED
	Total	Monthly	
Retirement			
Financial Independence			
College Education			
Pay Off All Debt			
Major Purchase			
Significant Change In Lifestyle			

Remember that Table 2.1 is a simple goal matrix and that you can add as many categories as you like. The categories are based on your own personal situation. Table 2.2 includes more details.

Appendix

Table 2.2 • A Detailed Goal Matrix

GOAL	Year 1	Year 1-5	Year 6-10	Year 11-30
Vacation				
New Home				
Pay Debts				
Income Property				
Child Care				
Fur Coat				
New Business				
Charity				
Other				
Other				
Other				
Other				
Other				

Table 3.1 • Monthly Budget

INCOME & EXPENSE STATEMENT

Month _____

INCOME

Payroll	_____
Commission	_____
Bonus	_____
Savings	_____
Investment	_____
Rental	_____
Business	_____
Other	_____
Other	_____

EXPENSES

Taxes	_____
Tithes	_____
Investments/Savings	_____
Mortgage/Rent	_____
Auto	_____
Credit/Loans	_____
Child Care	_____
Food/Groceries	_____
Clothing	_____
Transportation	_____
Insurance	_____
Medical	_____
Payroll Deduction	_____
Toiletries	_____
Recreation	_____
Miscellaneous	_____

TOTAL INCOME _____ **TOTAL EXPENSES** _____

SURPLUS OR DEFICIT = INCOME − EXPENSES _____

Table 3.6 • Balance Sheet

BALANCE SHEET

Date _____

ASSETS		LIABILITIES	
Cash (Reserve) Assets		**Short-Term Debts**	
Checking	_____	Credit Cards	_____
Savings and Money Markets	_____	Lines of Credit	_____
		Personal Loans	_____
Cash Value of Life Insurance Policy	_____	Margin Loans	_____
		Property Taxes	_____
Investment Assets			
Stocks, Bonds, and Mutual Funds	_____	**Long-Term Debts**	
		Auto Loans	_____
Retirement/ Keogh Accounts	_____	Student Loans	_____
Pension/401(k) (Vested)	_____	Mortgage Loan	_____
		Business Loans	_____
Personal Assets		Other	_____
Car	_____		
Furniture and Appliances	_____		
Jewelry, Other	_____		
Real Estate			
Home	_____		
Investment Property	_____		
Other Property	_____		
TOTAL ASSETS	_____	**TOTAL LIABILITIES**	_____

NET WORTH (Total=Assets–Liabilities) _____

Sample # 1 To Request A Copy Of Your Credit Report

Credit Bureau Name   Date
Consumer Relations Department
Street Address
City, State, Zip

Dear Credit Administrator:

Please send a copy of my credit report.

Your name: last, first, middle initial
Generation: (Jr., III, etc.)
Spouse's first name
Current address
Previous address
Year of birth
Social Security number

I have included a recent copy of my utility bill to verify my address. I would appreciate your immediate assistance in this matter.

Sincerely,

(Your signature)

Please send to: Name
                       Address
                       City, State, Zip

Sample # 2   To Request A Copy Of Your Credit Report Following Credit Denial

Credit Bureau Name   Date
Consumer Relations Department
Street Address
City, State, Zip

Dear Credit Administrator:

I was denied credit on (date) by (name of creditor) because of information on my credit report. Please send a copy of my credit report.

Your name: last, first, middle initial
Generation: (Jr., III, etc.)
Spouse's first name
Current address
Previous address
Year of birth
Social Security number

I would appreciate your immediate assistance in this matter.

Sincerely,

(Your signature)

Please send to: Name
                        Address
                        City, State, Zip

SAMPLE #3   To Dispute Accounts On Your Credit Report

Credit Bureau Name   Date
Consumer Relations Department
Address
City, State, Zip

Dear Credit Administrator:

In reviewing my credit report, I discovered accounts that are inaccurate. I am requesting that the following accounts be investigated and verified:

Creditor's name:
Creditor (subscriber) code:
Account number:
Reason for dispute:
* (You can include more than one account on this letter)

I understand that according to the Fair Credit Reporting Act (Section 611), the above request will be investigated and I will be notified of your results within thirty (30) days. Please send an updated copy of my credit report when you complete your investigation.

Your name: last, first, middle initial
Generation: (Jr., III, etc.)
Spouse's first name:
Current address:
Previous address:
Year of birth:
Social Security number:

I would appreciate your immediate assistance in this matter.

Sincerely,

(Your signature)

Please send to: Name
                         Address
                         City, State, Zip

Sample #4   **To Request Removal Of Credit Information Older Than 7 Years**

Credit Bureau Name   Date
Consumer Relations Department
Address
City, State, Zip

Dear Credit Administrator:

I have recently received a copy of my credit report. The following account(s) have had no transactions for seven years or more.

Creditor name:
Creditor (Subscriber) code:
Account number:
* (You can include more than one account on this letter)

My credit report shows a derogatory remark on this account. Under the Fair Credit Reporting Act (Sections 605-607), the statute of limitations has expired, and this account should be deleted from my credit report. Please delete the following account(s) and send an updated copy of my report.

Your name: last, first, middle initial
Generation: (Jr., III, etc.)
Spouse's first name:
Current address:
Previous address:
Year of birth:
Social Securit:y number

I would appreciate your immediate assistance in this matter.

Sincerely,

(Your signature)

Please send to: Name
                      Address
                      City, State, Zip

Sample # 5   To Place A Consumer Statement On Your Credit Report

Credit Bureau Name   Date
Consumer Relations Department
Address
City, State, Zip

Dear Credit Administrator:

Upon recently reviewing my credit report, I discovered an account that needs explanation and am requesting that the following consumer statement be added to my report.

Creditor name:
Creditor (subscriber) code:
Account number:
Consumer statement: _____
_____
_____
_____

* (You can include more than one account on this letter)

Your name: last, first, middle initial
Generation: (Jr., III, etc.)
Spouse's first name:
Current address:
Previous address:
Year of birth:
Social Security number:

I would appreciate your immediate assistance in this matter.

Sincerely,

(Your signature)
Please send to: Name
                        Address
                        City, State, Zip

Table 5.1 • Risk Tolerance Grid

Of the total amount of funds you have to save and invest, what percentage (%) would you prefer to invest in each category?

#1 Prefer Safest Investments (Lowest Risk/Lowest Return)	#2 Prefer Moderately Safe Investments With Little Risk (Low To Medium Risk and Return)
% of investments desired here _____	% of investments desired here _____
#3 Occasional Risk (Medium To High Risk and Return)	#4 Earn The Highest Return Possible No Matter What The Risk (Highest Risk and Return)
% of investments desired here _____	% of investments desired here _____

Table 6.1 • Monthly Principal and Interest Payment

1. Total monthly gross income $ _____

2. Multiply by the qualifying percentage (36%)   +   .36*

3. Amount of income available for monthly payments   = $ _____

4. Subtract current total monthly loan payments   – $ _____

(Credit cards, car payments, consumer loans, etc.)

5. Total monthly payment you may qualify for   = $ _____

6. Deduct monthly taxes and insurance** $ _____

7. Monthly principal and interest payment after taxes and insurance   = $ _____

*Your monthly debt payments should not exceed 36% of your monthly gross income.

**Amounts vary by location. Use 15% of line 5 as an estimate if you don't know the exact figure.*

Table 6.2 • Monthly Principal and Interest Payments

Interest Rate	6%	6.5%	7%	7.5%	8%	8.5%	9%
APR*	6.093%	6.596%	7.099%	7.602%	8.105%	8.609%	9.112%
Mortgage Amount	\multicolumn{7}{c}{Monthly Payment}						
$60,000	$360	$380	$400	$420	$441	$462	$483
$80,000	$480	$506	$533	$560	$588	$616	$644
$100,000	$600	$633	$666	$700	$734	$769	$805
$120,000	$720	$759	$799	$840	$881	$923	$966
$140,000	$840	$885	$932	$979	$1,028	$1,077	$1,127
$180,000	$1,080	$1,138	$1,198	$1,259	$1,321	$1,385	$1,449
$220,000	$1,320	$1,391	$1,464	$1,539	$1,615	$1,692	$1,771

APR Annual Percentage Rate, or the actual annual cost of credit. The APR represents the total finance charge (interest, loan fees, and points) as a percentage of the total loan amount.

THE URBAN GUIDE
ANSWER KEY

Chapter 1

1.) True Wealth includes all of the gifts, talents and spiritual riches that God has given you in addition to the monetary and material goods he has made available to you.

2.) He gave them land.

3.) Real estate.

4.) We can benefit from real estate as an asset through 1.) appreciation = the increase in its value over time, 2.) collecting rental income when leasing all of part of the property to others, 3.) And through tax reduction because one can deduct property taxes from one's gross income.

5.) Time, talent money and land.

6.) Time was used to enable the stewards to prepare and prove themselves as able managers of what was given to them.

Talent was used to give the stewards a chance to use their know how and ability.

Money was used to test the how faithful the stewards would be.

Land was used to reward the stewards. With land they could generate more income.

7.) Stewardship is managing something that belongs to another.

8.) God can use money to bless us, teach us and show his awesome power in our lives.

9.) God used Joseph's ability to dream and interpret dreams to elevate him to save the nations around him including the foreign land in which he resided, as well as his own family.

Chapter 2

1.) God used the ant to teach us about planning ahead because if something so small with no human intelligence prepares for each winter then we as humans should even more prepare finances for the times ahead.

156 | *The Urban Guide Answer Key*

2.) A financial plan is a working document used to map out our goals and the strategies we will use to achieve them.

3.) Needs are basic day-to-day necessities, such as food, shelter, clothing and health insurance.

Wants are things one purchases to enhance the quality of life, such as transportation, clothing, housing, etc. The style or quality of item depends on one's preference and budget. Desires are things that enhance are lives but exceed needs and wants usually by price and magnitude, such as, exotic vacations, fur coats, etc.

4.) Dreams are a fond hope or aspiration, while goals are objectives that one strives to attain.

5.) Short-term goals are objectives one plans to or will reach within one year or less. Medium-term goals are objectives which can be accomplished within 1 to 5 years. Long-term goals that can be accomplished in 6 years or more.

6.) Discuss dreams, goals and then finances.

7.) Schedule periodic reviews of your financial plan with yourself, spouse, financial planner, CPA, children and stockbroker (where applicable).

8.) Monthly, quarterly or semi-annually. The greater the financial difficulties you face, the more frequently you will need to discuss and review, possibly weekly or biweekly until you have a handle on the challenges.

9.) Collect a list of candidates. Meet at least three people from the list. Ask each candidate for references. Don't pay too much attention to the title. Check the advisors background. Do not trust a person just because he or she is a friend or relative. Ask how and how much the advisor will be paid. Have advisor explain how their recommendations will help you achieve your goals.

Ask how you will determine if the investments are producing the results you need.

10.) You do.

11.) Either chart can be used to calculate amounts needed to reach your 3-year goal.

GOAL	AMOUNT NEEDED	DATE NEEDED
	Total/Monthly	
Arizona	$10,000/$277.78	3 years from today
Start-up money for business	$4,000/$111.11	3 years from today

Calculations: $10,000 / 36months = $277.78 $4,000 / 36 months = $111.11

The Urban Guide Answer Key | 157

12.)

GOAL	YEAR 1	YEAR 1-5	YEAR 6-10	11-30+
Ann/Mon	Ann/Mon	Ann/Mon	Ann/Mon	Ann/Mon
New Car	$9,600/$400			
Braces	$1,750/$146			
Private School	$3,000/$250			
Your Education	$10,000/$1,111			

Payments on the new car will start in 2 years at $400/month. You will start saving $146/month immediately for one full year so that you will be able to pay for the braces at the time of service. You will save $250/month for four years which will add up to $3,000 a year, or a total of $12,000, which will cover tuition for four years of private school for your daughter. For your education it will cost you $10,000/year after your employer's 50% tuition reimbursement or $40,000 for four years, starting four years from now. You choose to start paying for your college education now by putting away $1,111.11/month for the next three years. This adds up to the $40,000 you will need to cover your tuition for four years.

The goal matrices above could have been set up in various ways. The answers above only reflect one way of handling these matters. No investment return or savings account interest was used for simplicity sake.

Chapter 3

1.) The monthly budget shows how much income was generated, how much was paid in expenses and how much surplus or deficit was left at the end of the month.

2.) Payroll, Mortgage, Auto Payment, Taxes and Rent are fixed. Commission, Investment, Grocery, Clothing and Toiletries are variable.

3.) So that we will save on a consistent basis (monthly or bi-weekly) to make sure that we have enough to pay these bills without creating an emergency and so we won't overspend.

4.) Add up the income categories and the expense categories separately, then subtract total expenses from total income to get your surplus or deficit amount.

5.) Emergency Fund, Cash Reserve, Gas, Dry Cleaning and Dental.

6.) The balance sheet shows assets (how much you own), liabilities (how much you owe) and net worth (how much you are worth).

7.) Cash assets, investment assets, personal assets and real estate assets.

8.) Short-term liabilities and long-term liabilities.

9.) Net worth = Assets - Liabilities

10.) An emergency fund is a savings that you build up to help you through financial challenges that may arise in your life. On the budget sheet one could increase the amounts that go into savings and investments and decrease the amount of credit and loans. On the balance sheet one could increase the amount placed in savings and money market accounts since these do not have specific time frames for which monies have to stay on deposit. When an emergency arises, you need money quick.

11.) The Jacksons can increase the amount that goes into their savings by $300/month and cut back spending $150/month in the Clothing category and $150/month in the Credit/Loan category. They could alternatively choose to cut back a total of $300 per month on Clothing or on the Credit/loan category. The couple chooses to increase the savings category versus investments because they need the funds as readily available as possible in an account that does not fluctuate in value with the market.

12.) See budget sheet.

Chapter 4

1.) Character, favor and position.

2.) Pay all bills in a timely manner. Check your credit history periodically with all three credit reporting agencies.

3.) Don't ignore financial problems when they arise, handle them swiftly. Avoid replacing needs with wants and desires when shopping. Set aside a reserve fund to help avoid overspending when emergencies and financial events arise, and to avoid using credit cards.

4.) Taking on additional employment is one strategy individuals can use to generate income to pay off debts. One should be careful however not to over-commit and create conflicts with family and the full-time job. One can borrow funds from their Employee Savings Plan at a lower rate than the banks offer and use this to pay off debts. Just remember that your employer will set up a payment plan that deducts a designated payment from your paycheck. Home equity loans can be used to pay off debts, while also receiving a tax deduction. One must use caution and make payments in a timely manner because one could lose their home if payments are not made timely.

5.) One can stop aggravating creditor calls by writing a cease-and-desist letter to the creditor informing them not to contact you again.

6.) Creditors cannot: harass, use a false name, give false credit information about you or use profane language.

7.) Creditors must identify themselves and the name of their company. Tell why they are calling, the amount you owe and the account. Send you a letter within 5 business days after they first contact you, giving you the creditor's name, how much you owe, and instructions to follow if the information is incorrect.

8.) Ask if you can may lower monthly payments for a few months. Ask if the creditor can extend the length of your loan to make lower monthly loan payments. Ask creditor if you can defer your payments for 30, 60 or 90 days, especially with auto loans. For charged-off accounts, offer the collection agency 25% of the original balance owed.

9.) Request a copy of your credit report from all three credit reporting agencies and review the status of your credit. Write to the credit bureau(s) if you find inaccurate information on your report. Check your report for delinquent accounts that are more than 7 years old. These accounts cannot be kept on your report if no transactions (payments or purchases) have been made. Dispute the inaccuracy of any erroneous information on your credit report and if the credit reporting bureau (agency) doesn't respond in 30 days, they must remove the derogatory information from your report.

10.) Equifax, Experian and Trans Union.

11.) Set up payment arrangements with your creditor for yourself, without bankruptcy court involvement.

12.) Get the bankruptcy discharged as soon as possible by paying off debts sooner than scheduled. Accelerate the payments by sending additional money to the creditor whenever possible. Set up additional savings to pay off creditors sooner. Generate extra income through part-time work, additional hours on the job, small business, etc., to pay debts off faster.

13.) Consumer Credit Counseling, Money Management International and Debtors Anonymous.

Chapter 5

1.) They are destroyed.

2.) Knowledge helps you to avoid roadblocks that could destroy your future.

3.) Category 1 = Checking account & money market account. Category 2 = Utility stocks & blue chip stocks. Category 3 = Small cap mutual funds & High yield bond funds. Category 4 = Options & Gold.

4.) Because Mrs. Barnes has no other indicated source of income and is in her 60's, she cannot afford to take any risk. 80% of her funds should be put into category 1 and 20% should be put into category 2.

5.) Because Frank and Eleanor's daughter has 11 years before she attends college they could put 100% of the monthly investment into category 3, or 80% in category 3 and 20% in category 2. Short-term market fluctuations won't matter as much because the stock market has historically performed well over longer periods of time.

6.) Income stocks provide investors with a consistent dividend with little fluctuation in price per share. Growth stocks provide investors with the most opportunity to receive high return on investment, though growth is not guaranteed.

Municipal bonds are long-term, tax-exempt securities that represent a loan to state or local governments and their agencies. Zero coupon bonds are a form of fixed income debt that owe their name to the fact that they do not bear coupons that can be redeemed for interest.

International funds invest in stocks that are traded on foreign exchanges. Sector funds invest in a specific industry such as biotechnology or oil stocks.

Savings accounts are no-risk, low-interest accounts that can be established with a bank or credit union for an indefinite period of time, with unrestricted withdrawals or deposits. Money market accounts are no-risk accounts, with minimum check-writing privileges, and a higher balance and interest than both a checking and a savings account.

7.) Initial public offerings are stocks made available to the public by companies that are going public for the first time. These stocks are usually sold through brokerage companies.

Direct Public Offerings are stocks that are sold directly to the public by a corporation.

8.) Options, futures and precious metals.

9.) Above maximum income levels you cannot qualify to make contributions to a Roth IRA but you can still contribute to a traditional IRA account at any income level.

10.) With the *Uniform Gift Transfer to Minors Act* the child has control of the funds when they turn 18. With the Education IRA the parents has control of the funds when the child turns 18.

11.) 401k is a salary reduction plan that allows as higher contributions than an IRA. 403(b) is a salary deduction plan offered to employees of non-profit organizations.

12.) The difference between a full-service, discount and online broker are the fees they charge and the form of communication they use. Full-service brokers can advise individuals on various investment types and strategies, and charge the highest commission of the three. A discount broker can handle buy and sell orders but cannot give advice, with a commission fee that much less than a full-service broker but ore than the cost of an online broker. An online broker handles computerized buy and sell orders from clients via the Internet, with no verbal contact with the customer. As a result, their commission fee is much lower than a full-service or discount broker.

13.) Buy and sell securities, research investments and receive quotes.

14.) Mutual fund   20% - 3% = 17% (Actual return)
      High yield bond   11% - 3% = 8% (Actual return)
      Money market account   5% - 3% = 2% (Actual return)

Chapter 6

1.) The people were told to be strong and courageous. This was necessary because they had to go and take possession of their land from other people.

2.) Planning ahead, budgeting, maintaining good credit habits, and using appropriate investments to save for future goals. We additionally need to seek out wise counsel from a legal advisor, real estate agent and appraiser.

3.) Rental income, tax advantages and security.

4.) Total monthly gross income, current monthly loan payments and monthly taxes and insurance.

5.) Pre-qualification is the process of calculating the loan amount you can qualify for. Pre-approval is being approved for a specific loan amount, for which you receive a commitment letter from a mortgage company.

6.) Loan origination fee, credit report fee, prepaid mortgage insurance, property survey fee, deed recording fee, attorney's fee and property inspection fee.

7.) $100,000 * 3% (.03) = $3,000 $100,000 * 5% (.05) = $5,000

     $3,000 + $5,000 = $8,000 (Amount needed to close).

8.) Prepare a list of your needs and wants, pre-qualify you for a home, help find suitable financing and schedule appointments to view homes/property.

9.) Government mortgages allow for down payments as low as 3% and in some cases nothing down (for veterans).

10.) A 203 (k) mortgage loan is an FHA loan that provides funds for both home financing and renovation.

11.) The sub-prime mortgage lender generally handles borrowers who have current credit problems or has faced such problems in the past.

12.) Residential rental property contains two to four units and can be financed with a traditional mortgage loan. Commercial rental property contains six or more units and must be financed with a commercial loan.

13.) Surrounding Area—Neighborhood, property values and major highways.
      Property Exterior—Roof, walls and garage.
      Property Interior—Floor plan, plumbing and electrical system.

14.) www.century21.com and www.remax.com.

Chapter 7

1.) Performing our work faithfully can open up doors of opportunity for us.

2.) A sole proprietorship a business owned by one person, who may also be the only employee. A partnership is a business that gives several individuals control of the business, based on percentages set forth in the partnership agreement. A corporation is a business which has a management team that run the day-to-day operations. It also has a board of directors that is responsible for hiring and firing the management team. Lastly, it has shareholders who invest in the business. In a small business you can take on each of these roles.

3.) **Sole proprietorship**
Advantages—Easy to start, less government regulation All profits go to sole proprietor.

Disadvantages—Unlimited personal liability, difficult to raise money and Sole proprietor has to do all jobs necessary to remain in business.

Partnership
Advantages—Additional money can be invested by partners, better decision-making ability exists with more partners and Can spread workload to gain more efficiency in operations.

Disadvantages—Legal fees are higher than those for a sole proprietorship, it can be difficult to get rid of a bad partner and bankruptcy or other financial hardships of one partner can endanger the survival of the business.

Corporation
Advantages—The shareholder/owner has limited liability, you can raise money through shareholders and You can maintain control of you company.

Disadvantages—Most costly form of business, it is the most complicated form of business to run and it is challenging to find financing for new businesses.

4.) **Sole Proprietorship**
Income tax, self-employment tax and state sales taxes for those selling products.

Partnership
Income tax, self-employment tax and state sales tax if products are sold.

Corporation
Personal income tax, corporate tax and tax on dividends to shareholders.

5.) A percentage of your home utilities, maintenance fees, mortgage payments, rent and assessments.

Additionally you can take deductions for your car, office equipment and supplies purchased for your business.

6.) The IRS allows you to deduct certain portions of business assets (things you own) over a specific period of time.

7.) $40,000/5 years = $8,000/year can be deducted.

Chapter 8

1.) They leave an inheritance.

2.) Because one needs to know how much money would be needed to survive a death or disability and the loss of income that would result from these events.

3.) Renewable term insurance can be renewed every year, with premiums that increase every year.

Level term life insurance policies have premium payments that are fixed for the entire term of the policy.

4.) Whole, Universal and Variable life.

5.) $50,000 + $15,000 = $65,000 * 8% (.08) = $5,200

6.) Cash value policies carry a death benefit plus tax-deferred savings, term policies have no savings feature.

7.) With variable life you can decide how your money will be invested, with whole life the insurance company decides where your money is invested.

8.) A will is a legal document that transfers what you own to your beneficiaries when you die, designates the funds or assets that should be used to pay off your estate and inheritance taxes, and names the executor who will handle carrying out the terms of your will.

9.) The guardian handles your children. The trustee manages the assets in your estate.

10.) An estate plan allows you to design a comprehensive plan using gifts, trusts and other strategies to disburse your assets.

11.) The estate plan includes everything (asset) in your name, half of everything you own jointly with your spouse and all that you own jointly with another person.

12.) Bypass trusts allow you to pass up to $600,000 tax-free on to your heirs after your survivng spouse's death.

Chapter 9

1.) Jesus' point was that we all must pay taxes.

2.) To reduce taxes.

3.) Monetary and non-monetary contributions.

4.) Mileage to church, choir robe purchases, dry-cleaning of choir robes and travel expenses.

5.) Using your home for small business, purchasing real estate for depreciation and Using equity lines and loans to make purchases.

6.) This is a small business deduction. Travel, entertainment and lodging can be claimed as deductions.

7.) Rent, business fees and investment income.

8.) 3 - 7 years.

9.) Agents charge fees between $100 - $300, are certified by the U.S. Treasury Department and accredited by the IRS. CPAs are Certified Public Accountants who are specially trained to handle your accounting and tax matters and can charge $500 - $2,500 depending on the clients situation.

10.) How much it will cost to prepare your return. Is tax advisor available all year around? What kind of training does the tax advisor have? Does advisor have experience with tax situations similar to yours?